Heav'n's First Law

Heav'n's First Law

RHETORIC AND ORDER

IN POPE'S *ESSAY ON MAN*

Martin Kallich, *1918 –*

NORTHERN ILLINOIS UNIVERSITY PRESS

DeKalb

ACKNOWLEDGMENT

Papers On Literature & Language, Southern Illinois University, Edwardsville: for two essays entitled "Unity and Dialectic: The Structural Role of Antithesis in Pope's *Essay on Man,*" PLL, I, 2 (1965) and "The Conversation and the Frame of Love: Images of Unity in Pope's *Essay On Man,*" PLL, II, 1 (1966).

Preface

"... a general map of man"

AN ESSAY ON MAN, "The Design"

THE THOUGHT of Alexander Pope's *An Essay on Man* (1733-34) has been exhaustively treated by commentators from Bishop Warburton in the mid-eighteenth century to Professor Mack in the twentieth. Lately, however, some attention is being paid to subordinate sections of the work as poetry. This shift in focus is in accord with a trend that favors studies in the rhetoric of literature. No careful examination of the whole work as poem, particularly with regard to the structural function of its rhetoric, has yet been made. The four sections gathered together here attempt to fill this gap in Pope scholarship.

The method employed in these analyses is simple. Pope, like all poets who have written a good deal, favors certain stylistic devices or modes of expression and conceptualizes by means of word repetition. One essay is an attempt to show how the antithesis — after Joseph Warton's strictures thought to be the most characteristic of all of Pope's stylistic devices, the signature of his verse, so to speak — has been used to integrate the total poem and to provide certain special esthetic effects. Another essay focuses on repeated words and ideas — "right," "Providence," "bless" and its cognates — to show how Pope develops his argument and at the same time unifies the philosophy underlying the structure of the total poem. A third essay focuses on repeated imagery and attempts to reveal a pattern — the circular frame — that serves to unify the total poem at the same time that it makes vivid its visual effects.

The method of these studies is perhaps too simple and crude for the subtlety, density, and complexity that characterize Pope's poetry at its best. But that it has yielded some fruitful results, some new insights into the operations of Pope's imagination, is an empirical test of its validity. The value of these results the reader must judge for himself.

Each essay is distinct in so far as it deals with a special rhetorical problem, and each may be considered as a self-contained unit. But the cumulative effect of all the sections and their varying emphases — as suggested in the part summarizing the imagery in the *Essay on Man*—provide overwhelming testimony of the power and variety of Pope's poetic genius. It is hoped that these four essays add a little to the sum of knowledge about Pope's skill as an artist and thereby contribute to a finer appreciation and enjoyment of his poetry. Pope is lavish in his use of detail; this conclusion is borne out by intensive analysis of his imagery. Pope likewise demonstrates control; and this conclusion is supported by the evidence of the several different ways he has unified his great poem. In his "Epistle to Mr. Jervas" (1. 12), Pope himself describes this quality of his imagination: "so regular my rage." According to the norms of his own time, Pope married judgment and fancy in a decorous and seemly union; and according to the norms of a later day, including ours, he also exhibits the operations of a synthesizing and organic imagination.

CONTENTS

I

PROVIDENCE, SALVATION, AND BLISS

"Whatever is, is Right."

AN ESSAY ON MAN, I, 294

Pope once quoted "with great applause" the following passage from a sermon that he had been reading: "Where mystery begins, religion ends." Bolingbroke, whose attention was drawn to this remark, infers from Pope's attitude that "it shows an inclination, at least, to purify Christianity from the leaven of artificial theology, which consists principally in making things that are very plain, mysterious; and in pretending to make things, that are impenetrably mysterious, very plain."[1] No doubt, Pope would have agreed with Bolingbroke. For if *An Essay on Man* may be taken as a formal declaration of his credo, Pope justifies his religious faith not by means of inspiration and supernatural or miraculous mysteries but by means of an objective study of man's mind and those of its limitations which prevent man from explaining the natural mysteries in God's creation. In the same letter to Pope, Bolingbroke expressed this reasonable attitude effectively:

To be contented to know things as God has made us capable of knowing them, is then a first principle necessary to secure us from falling into error . . . God is hid from us in the majesty of his nature, and the little we discover of him, must be discovered by the light that is reflected from his works. Out of this light,

3

therefore, we should never go in our enquiries
and reasonings about his nature, his attributes,
and the order of his providence.[2]

Like Bolingbroke, Pope asserts a theism based upon
an empirical study of "what we know" (I, 17),[3] the
evidences of God in nature. Such study of what
appeared to him to be the clear facts of nature led
to the fundamental tenet of his religion, a God
with attributes of infinite goodness, wisdom, and
perfection; a tenet that he summed up in the simple
and luminously plain statement of faith in the
order of this God's Providence — "Whatever is, is
right."

In *An Essay on Man*, then, faith does not mean
explicit assent to biblical revelations that are supernatural and miraculous. Pope does not in the *Essay*
write of evidences of revealed religion, Old and New
Testament miracles, the incarnation of the Messiah
and his martyrdom, the doctrines of the Trinity
and the resurrection, free will and original sin, the
depravity of man, justification by faith or remission
of sins, grace, atonement, redemption, salvation,
and the efficacy of prayer.[4] As Pope confessed to
Joseph Spence, he deliberately altered his original
plan in order to avoid touching on ecclesiastical
government, by which he meant religious or sectarian doctrines: ". . . this was what chiefly stopped
my going on. I could not have said what I would
have said, without provoking every church on the

face of the earth; and I did not care for living always in boiling water."[5] On the other hand, the sort of faith that the *Essay* does recognize is that revelation of God in his natural works, in the order and harmony, goodness and perfection of the creation. It follows from these assumptions of Pope's system that man is denied redemption or salvation in the conventional Christian sense, and therefore he need not seek grace in order to be freed from the guilt or penalty of sin. Pope's re-interpretation of grace, salvation, and sin is in accordance not with conventional theological but with unorthodox and personal norms, those of his private system.

As a matter of fact, although the principal articles of the poet's confession in the poem are few and emphatically ethical, and in their orientation deistic, still it may be correct to state that in *An Essay on Man* Pope has made a personal declaration of religious faith — a faith in God and in the moral universe, epitomized in the optimism of "Whatever is, is right." This cosmic faith provides the frame for Pope's religious attitude which, as it is expressed in the *Essay* and in letters that parallel the sentiments of the poem, exhibit him as basically a sensitive, charitable, broadminded person.

[i]

What Pope wishes to do in the *Essay*, it is clear, is to focus on first principles, the grounds of religion in nature. He accepts as the bases of philosophy, natural theology or theism, natural religion or ethics, two axioms, as formulated by Bolingbroke: "those self-evident, and necessary truths alone, of which we have an immediate perception, since they are not confined to any special parts of science, but are common to several, or to all. Thus these profitable axioms, What is, is; The whole is bigger than a part. . . ."[6] Precisely these are the fundamental theses adopted by Pope — they are the footings upon which the edifice of his thought rests. The first axiom indicates a recognition of the material universe of which man is but an infinitesimal part, and suggests that man, essentially helpless to alter nature, must resign himself to accept things as they are in the structured infinite. The second indicates a recognition that parts constitute a whole and implies that the limitations of being finite prevent the part from ever comprehending the infinity characteristic of the immense whole. Resignation and humility — such are the implications of these axioms.

Pope does not read a cynical or stoical pessimism into these spiritual attitudes. Significantly in the last line of Epistle I (perhaps following Shaftesbury), he adds the word "right" to Bolingbroke's first axiom, making explicit the absolute benevolence of the universe and implying the governing power of a perfect wisdom over it.[7] Pope's own

marginal comment on this line in the manuscript
of the poem tells us what he thought he meant:
"Thy will be done, in Earth as it is in Heaven."[8]
Pope, here as in "The Universal Prayer" (line 48),
is simply adapting the Lord's Prayer in *Matthew*,
6:9-15, and humbly submitting to divine Providence. Thus the famous declaration effectively
sums up the underlying optimism of Pope's creed
that is certainly not inconsistent with Christianity.
This optimistic faith must have meant a good deal
to Pope, both intellectually and spiritually. For he
employs it to "vindicate the ways of God to Man"
(I, 16) in abstract metaphysical argument and to
allay personal anxieties, as he expresses his belief
in God's goodness and wisdom in these words —
or in words very much like them — again and
again in the *Essay on Man* and at moments of
domestic crisis such as sickness, suffering, and
death.[9]

Further, with regard to the *Essay*, to illustrate
the thematic importance of God's Providence, Pope
uses it to structure the total work. In the first
epistle, his major concern is to consider man with
respect to the universe; in the second, with respect
to himself; in the third, with respect to society; in
the fourth, with respect to his moral values. But
in none of these does Pope ever lose sight of man
in his relationship to God and His Providence.[10]
Each epistle concludes with an assertion of faith

in the divine perfection, goodness, or wisdom.

The basic argument of the first epistle rests upon the assumptions that God intentionally chose the best world for man and that He systematized the infinite abundance of the natural universe by means of "the great chain, that draws all to agree" (I, 33). Thus, as the word "agree" suggests, the variety of things in nature are harmoniously fitted to each other, exist together without conflict, and exhibit no inequalities or discordances, in terms of the perfect order that the natural system as a whole possesses. According to this system, therefore, the particular is necessarily evil or imperfect but becomes good or perfect as it functions in the general whole; or, to express this idea in Pope's manner, partial evil tends to universal good, whatever human beings think is wrong in their private world is really right relative to the whole, the infinite abundance of the universe of nature: "Whatever wrong we call, / May, must be right, as relative to all" (I, 51-52). Human beings have no cause for complaint, simply because, as Pope concludes, "Whatever is, is right" (I, 294). Pope's gloss for this notable declaration, which cogently epitomizes the thought of the first epistle, is a resolute statement of faith in God's Providential plan for the present and future: "The consequence of all, the absolute submission due to Providence, both as to our present and future state" (Argument, I, x).

By "right," it is clear, Pope means the disposition of God, or Providence, that makes everything in the universe, even evil itself, tend to the greater perfection of the whole.[11] Thus Pope adapts and combines Bolingbroke's two axioms in his view of a just and benign Providence.

Similarly, the other epistles stress the benevolent and ordering role of God's Providence, demonstrating its unifying structural function in the total poem. In the second, Pope concludes with an assertion of divine wisdom: "Tho' Man's a fool, yet God is Wise" (II, 294). For God has so disposed and synthesized the disordered passions of individual men that society as a whole benefits, a happy result explicated by Pope in his prose Argument with an explicit reference to Providence: " . . . the Ends of Providence and general Good are answered in our Passions and Imperfections" (II, vi). In the third, Pope demonstrates how Providence operates in government and religion. Thus evil ultimately becomes good, as "God and Nature . . . bade Self-love and Social be the same" (III, 317-18). In the fourth, Pope defines lasting happiness in terms of virtue and relates it to the divine order. Again, the gloss in the Argument clearly relates man's virtue to the general goal of Providence: "That Virtue only constitutes a Happiness, whose object is universal, and whose prospect eternal. That the perfection of Virtue and

Happiness consists in a conformity to the Order of
Providence here, and a Resignation to it here and
hereafter" (IV, vii). The echo of the Lord's Prayer
is, it should be noted, unmistakable.

Obviously, because of its important structural
function, the keystone to Pope's natural theology
is his conception of God's Providence, the principle
central to his profession of religion in the *Essay on
Man*. Its definition illuminates Pope's meaning of
just exactly what is "right" with the world. The
common view of Providence, what Pope describes
as "The great directing Mind of All" (I, 266), declares its divine guidance and care, which, in turn,
implies that the administration of God is wise and
good, the natural creation purposeful and orderly.[12]
Moreover, Providence is impartial or general. That
is to say, according to Pope's argument, "the first
Almighty Cause / Acts not by partial, but by
gen'ral laws" (I, 145-46). Thus, again, man's
limited intelligence classifies catastrophes such as
plagues, earthquakes, and tidal waves or tempests
as evils, but that is so only because man cannot see
their end. This principle is even used to explain
the mysterious manner by which the diversity of
passions are by God accommodated to each other
in a coherent society: "Heav'n's great view is One,
and that the Whole" (II, 238). And this general
and overall perspective, which only the deity has,
permits Pope, as noted before, to assert the omni-

science of God (II, 294).

Unfortunately, however, man cannot entirely comprehend the universe of nature and its general laws because of physical and mental shortcomings. Indeed, to what ultimate purpose Providence does operate is a complete mystery to man — and the frank assertion of this mystery is precisely Pope's major theme in the *Essay*, the source of its controversial quality. For Pope, believing with Bolingbroke that the full definition of the divine order and purpose is ultimately unknowable to man in his present condition, vigorously writes against those who think they know. These people, he frequently tells us, are such as "Weigh [their] Opinion against Providence" (I, 114), and criticize the government of God for the supposed imperfections they think they see in nature. Such men, proud and impious, are "blind to truth, and God's whole scheme below" (IV, 93). Really, man's limitations are quite proper to his station in the whole scheme of things: "Who finds not Providence all good and wise, / Alike in what it gives, and what it denies?" (I, 205-06). In short, man must understand that God is "right"— that is, perfect, good, wise, and impartial — so far as His Providential acts demonstrate.

Lastly, in Pope's argument, not only natural catastrophes or physical evil but also the moral evil for which man himself is responsible are both

parts of God's overall plan, God's general Providence, and ultimately contribute thereby to perfection: "Account for moral, as for nat'ral things. /
Why charge we Heav'n in those [natural evils], in
these [moral acts of human beings] acquit? / In
both, to reason right is to submit" (I, 162-64).
Hence man must cease his restless questioning
and be content to submit to God's will as manifest
in the grand design of the universe, of which he
can perceive only a part. Clearly, what Pope is
driving at is an assertion of the difference between
real or ultimate good and apparent or temporary
evil, a difference which the "Eternal Wisdom"
(II, 29) can distinguish. In this context, "submit"
simply means that human beings must be content
and have faith in God's omniscience and omni-
potence as manifest in the universal order, natural
and human: For "The gen'ral Order . . . Is kept in
Nature, and is kept in Man" (I, 171-72). And,
with regard to the happiness of all mankind, it is
Providence, "Heav'n's just balance," that equalizes
apparent and particular inequalities in wealth, and
provides a general order for society; for those who
are fortunate live in fear while those who are not
live in hope (IV, 67-72). Once more, Pope expli-
cates this role of Providence in the Argument:
"notwithstanding the inequality, the balance of
Happiness among Mankind is kept even by Providence, by the two passions of Hope and Fear"

(IV, ii). With regard to the human moral order, Providence adjusts the parts to the needs of the whole so that all is "right" or just and perfect.

This complete faith in the Providential control of everything in the universe, natural and human, is the source of the charge of fatalism or naturalism (that is, the creed of natural religion) directed at the *Essay*. For example, Crousaz objects to the resignation implicit in the assertion, as he interprets it, that "what will be, will be; or whatever is, should be." A militant Roman Catholic, Crousaz insists upon the reality of free will and evil:

Why then does Mr. Pope aspire so high, reason so freely, and decide so boldly upon the greatest of all Subjects? If we take his Word, the supreme Bcing was inevitably determined to create *this* Universe because the most perfect that he could conceive, yet there is nothing perfect in that Part which is assigned for our Habitation; it is full of Imperfections, which God is the Author of, and could not avoid. He takes care not to proceed to the ill Use made by Man of his Liberty, the Original of all the Evil that surrounds us, suitably enough to that state of Disorder in which Men live by their own Fault.

. . . if the Submission, so strongly recommended as the sure Way to everlasting Happiness, consists in looking undisturb'd and careless upon every Thing that passes, in an indolent and supine Unconcern about our Ac-

tions and those of others, it is a fatal Calm, an ill-
grounded Security that tends to the total Overthrow
of Morality and Religion.[13]

So Pope, according to Crousaz's interpretation, appears to undermine the Christian doctrine of original sin, man's responsibility for bringing all evil
into the world. (These are also part of the Anglican
Confession — Articles 9 and 10.) But Pope is concerned not with man's free will but with God and
His will; and so his theism, despite this objection,
is unequivocal.[14] Insisting upon taking the view of
the divine absolutes, eternity and perfection, he
introduces another notion into his private religious
system, one that derives from his view of the Providential order and that rounds out his theology
and completes his definition of what constitutes
"right" in the universe.

[ii]

Providence, as we have seen, all wise, perfect,
and good, as well as impartial or general, operates
as the chief mystery of nature by giving an inex-
plicable order and purpose to the parts that constitute the whole of the universe, including man's
moral life. By means of its adjustments, Providence
makes whatever is absolutely right. But just exactly
how this order and purpose, this "right," should be
defined is a controversial matter. Some people cannot consider Providence perfect or complete without

the possibility of a state beyond mortal life in the eternal hereafter, so that the wrongs of this world may be redressed in the next. Others, like Pope and Bolingbroke, insist upon the perfection of the system as it is in the fixed chain of being without respect to the immortal hereafter for human beings —this being the Providence vindicated in *An Essay on Man*. But this position on a future life is not maintained consistently in the poem. Pope would have it both ways. Hence the ambiguity in his view of perfection, an ambiguity manifest in his use of the word "bless" and all its cognates — "blesses," "blessing," "blessed," and "bliss." These words are used so often — about fifty times[15]— in the *Essay* that the mere repetition, like that of "wit" in the *Essay on Criticism,* becomes significantly meaningful.

In the first epistle (I, 69-76), Pope insists in his initial discussion of this concept that man is "blest" simply in his present state — "Man's as perfect as he ought" to be, or "perfect in a certain sphere." According to Pope's view of the ways of Providence, man in his assigned state and place in the best of all possible worlds fits quite properly into the larger system and scheme of things and is thereby blessed. In this sense, Pope continues, everyone in the past or present is equally blessed. Thus Pope is careful to point out that he does not mean an exclusive salvation through Jesus; to be

blessed means contentment with what God has
given man in this life, and no more. For a significant characteristic of man in this condition is his
ignorance of the divine plan — he simply does not
know what lies in store for him beyond this state
after death: "Heav'n from all creatures hides the
Book of Fate" (I, 77).[16]

Although God withholds from man the knowledge of "future bliss" (I, 93), Pope here refers
to immortality, yet He has endowed man in the
mortal state with hope as his blessing — "gives
that Hope to be thy blessing now" (I, 94). It will
be seen that the word, in this new context, does not
have the old meaning of contentment with one's
station in this life. Playing with the word in the
next few lines, Pope gives it yet another meaning
— "Man never Is, but always To be blest" (I, 96).
Further, Pope continues, man's hope ought to be
natural, humble, charitable, like that of the simple
Indian who, not particularly exclusive, welcomes
his dog into the heavenly state, "a life to come"
(I, 98). Pope, it should be emphasized, does not
specifically admit that immortality is or should be
granted to man. He admits only that man, in accordance with his position in the chain of being,
may properly hope for it. Merely to hope is a
blessing granted by Providence. This idea he repeats in the second epistle: "Hope travels thro', nor
quits us when we die" (II, 274). But here, curi-

ously, he appears to go somewhat further than he
did in the first epistle — for such hope persists even
after death!

Up to this point in our discussion, we can see
that Pope gives three meanings to the word "blessing" — contentment with one's place in the divine
system (shall we call this a species of contingent
perfection or salvation?), hope for a life after death,
and, conventionally, exaltation or salvation in the
immortal state. These are the three referents that
cause whatever ambiguity there is in the religious
thought of the *Essay;* but the last notion is the
least significant in his system, except for the climax
of the fourth epistle.

To illustrate how exasperating this ambiguity
may become, a few lines after he gave man hope,
Pope unexpectedly denies the realization of this
hope, this possibility, when he asserts that man,
believing that God has singled him out for a special
dispensation, is in error. Man has no legitimate
complaint, Pope declares, if he is not singled out
for perfection on earth and immortality in heaven:
"If Man alone ingross not Heav'n's high care, /
Alone made perfect here, immortal there" (I, 119-
20). As already noted, the reason for God's impartiality is that His Providence operates by means
of general laws; to think otherwise is to suffer the
delusion of pride: "All quit their sphere, and rush
into the skies. / Pride still is aiming at the blest

abodes" (I, 124-25). So Pope ironically returns to
his first definition of "blest" meaning life in a certain sphere; for the heavenly abodes are, according
to the gradation of the great chain of being, properly the habitat of holy angels, genuinely spiritual
creatures, not earth-bound men. Interestingly
enough, Pope's hostility to such a notion is even
more emphatic in another context where, using the
very same expression, he declares that superstition
is responsible for the division of the after-world
into hell, "the dreadful," and heaven, "the blest
abodes" (III, 255).[17]

Bolingbroke and Pope thus agree that the eternal
blessing or salvation which grace may bring cannot
be man's in another state, the hereafter. It is impious for man to assume or demand such immortality for himself, because this implies a criticism
of God's supposed imperfections and, to boot, may
be evidence of superstition. The true blessing, Pope
reiterates, "The bliss of Man . . . Is not to act or
think beyond mankind" (I, 189-90), but to submit
to the law of his nature which, as already noted, is
perfect relative to the whole system of things.
Bolingbroke has effectively defined such human
happiness: " . . . man was not made to be happier
than it was consistent with this part of the material
System, and with his own rank in the intellectual,
that he should be." Man is blessed in this best of
possible worlds as much as his place in it calls for:

"It implys contradiction of God's infinite goodness and perfection to say that God should have made a creature infinitely happy, as happy as himself. But it implys none to say that he made a system of creation infinitely wise and the best of all possible systems." The most we can do is to hope for continued happiness in a future state, Bolingbroke declares, in words very much like Pope's:

He alone is happy, and he is truly so, who can say, welcome life whatever it brings! Welcome death whatever it is! "Aut transfert, aut finit." If the former, we change our state, but we are still the creatures of the same God. He makes us to be happy here. He may make us happier in another system of Being. At least, this we are sure of, we shall be dealed with according to the perfections of his nature, not according to the imperfections of our own. Resignation in this instance cannot be hard to one who thinks worthily of God, nor in the other, except to one who thinks too highly of man. . . . Let others be solicitous about their future state, and frighten, or flatter themselves as prejudice, imagination, bad health, or good health, nay a lowering day, or a clear sunshine shall inspire them to be. Let the tranquillity of my mind rest on this immoveable rock, that my future, as well as my present state are ordered by an Almighty and Allwise Creator; and that they are equally foolish, and presumptuous, who make imaginary excursions into futurity, and who complain of the present. [18]

Pope, like Bolingbroke, insists that man's consecrated role can only be considered perfect and complete in the same way that any part properly contributes to the smooth functioning of the machine
as a whole. Thus man can fulfill his unique destiny
in the Providential order: "In this, or any other
sphere, / Secure to be as blest as thou canst bear"
(I, 285-86).

In sum, Pope in the first epistle permits man two
types of felicity — those which possess the attributes of (1) security, contentment, resignation,
and (2) humble hope. Such is man's bliss; such
his perfection — when he accepts the system of
things as it is and his fixed position in it. But Pope
specifically denies man the ultimate blessing, the
third blessing, the heavenly joy characterized by
immortality or eternal salvation, for final knowledge of the meaning of death is not given to man
in his present state. More than once Pope satirizes
those men (presumably theologians like Samuel
Clarke with whom he and Bolingbroke took issue)
for their restless and subversive pride, that is, their
flat declaration that because this world contains
imperfections man requires the redemption of
Christ to achieve grace and immortal perfection.
To Pope, however, man is thus assuming the role
of Providence as he attempts to "Re-judge his
justice, be the God of God" (I, 122).

In the third epistle, Pope continues the discussion of his theme of hope, and thereby demonstrates again its importance to the thought of the poem. Pope declares that animals are unlike men in that Providence has not given them the useless knowledge of their end. Only man, through the unique endowment of reason, is imparted such knowledge, "As, while he dreads it, makes him hope it too" (III, 74). The point that Pope emphasizes is that man, of the whole creation the only creature with reason, possesses the gift of foreknowledge of his possible salvation in a future state of immortality, and can thereby make a fitting preparation for his reception there. Does this assumption of immortality appear to contradict his former remarks? Certainly, he seems to go beyond a declaration of hope. Perhaps cognizant of the danger of undermining his position so forcefully argued in the first epistle, Pope almost immediately withdraws from the temptation to speculate on the after-life and focuses once again on man's position in the universe in this life.

Therefore, when Pope states that man is endowed with a balance of reason and instinct, he returns to his first equation — that to be blessed means happiness in a certain sphere: "Whether with Reason, or with Instinct blest, / Know, all enjoy that pow'r which suits them best" (III, 79-80). The proper operation of each faculty, Pope asserts, will bring "bliss" (III, 82-83). Pope then uses this

conception of contentment with what Providence
offers to buttress the whole-part axiom as applied
to society. That is, each individual contributes to
the general welfare of the consecrated whole, the
divine perfection of society represented by the
chain of love. Thus Pope draws a parallel with the
chain of being, which he had used to support his
argument in the first epistle for man's special type
of blessing within a certain sphere.

> *God, in the nature of each being, founds*
> *Its proper* bliss, *and sets its proper bounds:*
> *But as he fram'd a Whole, the Whole to* bless,
> *On mutual Wants built mutual Happiness.*
> (III, 109-12)

But Pope has more to say about the blessed, perfect, or "right" state in the third epistle. The mono-
theistic patriarchs of old, Pope believes, had a
truly blessed civil society because they founded it
on natural love and benevolence. In this period,
Pope says, echoing the rhetoric of his philosophical
optimism, when man was in the state of nature,
"all was right," and genuine worship, "True faith,"
and good government, "true policy," were joined
(III, 232, 239). This image of natural religion, of
man simply worshipping a God whose chief attribute is love, is repeated at the end of the epistle.
The truly blessed society is one that rests on natu-

ral love — such is Pope's message. And its importance to the poet is made emphatic by means of its
climactic position in this epistle.

There Pope elaborates his view of true religion
in the state of nature when, as he says, "all was
right," blessed or perfect. Like a deist or broadminded latitudinarian, Pope minimizes sectarian
creeds, draws the lesson of a tolerant, stable, and
balanced government which "in proportion as it
blesses [is] blest" (III, 300), and then urges mankind to agree on the fundamental importance of
charity: for "all [must be] of God that bless Mankind or mend" (III, 310). On the other hand, however, "For Modes of Faith, let graceless zealots
fight" (III, 305). The depth of Pope's feeling is
indicated by the vehemence of his satire at this
point of his argument and by the harsh word
"graceless" taken from the vocabulary of Christian
polemics. To him, such people, like those whom he
had before castigated as proud, are not right and
do not deserve salvation, whatever that may mean
according to their own values. But charity, following the Apostle Paul's recommendations, Pope insists, genuinely partakes of the divine spirit and is
then, according to his system of values, the proper
course to beatification, the state of grace.[19] Pope,
it must be repeated, does not attempt to set up a
system for the exclusive salvation of those souls
redeemed by Jesus; on the contrary, he wishes to

set up a viable benevolent system for the salvation
of everyone who does good. His is the position of an
enlightened and sceptical moralist.

The theme of benevolence is repeated in the last
epistle, where in the climactic position it is given
great emphasis and rounds out the thought of the
whole work. He who understands God's "whole
scheme below" or "great scheme" that "partial Ill
is universal Good," Pope declares in the introduction of the fourth epistle, "Best knows the blessing,
and will most be blest" (IV, 93, 95-96, 114). So
Pope, ever concerned to unify his thought, argues
that man's genuine happiness, the subject of this
epistle, can come only through virtue, particularly
charity or love. The implications of a benevolent
Providence are thus developed in all the epistles.
Only virtue, Pope insists, is a constant source of
earthly happiness, "human bliss" (IV, 311), defined simply as charity which "Is blest in what it
takes, and what it gives" (IV, 314). This virtue,
"the sole bliss Heav'n could on all bestow" (IV,
327), is definitely not the exclusive property of any
religious sect, Pope insists again — "Slave to no
sect" (IV, 331). Indeed, the "height of Bliss" is
"but height of Charity" (IV, 360).

At this point getting at the heart of his religion
of ethics, Pope writes with a kind of exalted and
evangelical enthusiasm. The hope of the soul's
immortality that he had formerly held out for the

good man may now be strengthened by a faith in God (IV, 343), a faith that will permit man to experience the full "bliss" of everlasting felicity (IV, 344; Argument, IV vii: "A Happiness . . . whose prospect is eternal"). Only such a man understands why the species of "Man alone" (IV, 345) of all the creation has "Hope of known bliss" (IV, 346) — here Pope means the happiness and security that man achieves when he fits snugly, properly, and virtuously into God's benevolent system — and "Faith in bliss unknown" (IV, 346) — here (as in line 344) Pope accepts the conventional definition of "bliss" as endless heavenly joy. Such hope and faith, Pope states, combine in man "His greatest Virtue," which is love of God and submission to his benevolent authority, "With his greatest Bliss," which is the exalted happiness that one achieves in the immortal state (IV, 350). Thereby, as he loves God and practices virtue by being charitable to his fellows, man's everlasting life in the future is assured: "his own bright prospect to be blest" (IV, 351).[20] Such salvation, as noted before, does not come in Pope's system through the blood of the martyred Son of God — an omission, obviously congenial to Bolingbroke, of the Christian doctrine of miraculous atonement. But it is questionable whether Bolingbroke would have agreed with the article of faith encouraging belief in immortality, a mystery for which there is no verifiable evidence in nature.

It may very well be true that Pope, momentarily
carried away by rapturous prophetic vision, failed
to see that eternal salvation, in the conventional
Christian sense, is inconsistent with his message to
"erring Pride, Whatever is, is right," based on God's
Providence and nature and the limitations of man's
reason, the fact that "all our knowledge is, ourselves to know" (IV, 394, 398). Certainly, his ex-
tension of the knowledge of hope into the mystery
of faith at this point may be too strong, too positive, to be accommodated with the naturalistic
hypothesis of the first epistle. There, it will be re-
membered, Pope flatly denies the need of immortality for his theology and ethics; and there, and in
the other epistles as well, he declares that man in
his present state, unable to discover what happens
upon death, must be content with the hope which a
limited mortal reason entitles him to have.

With respect to this expression of faith at the
conclusion of the *Essay*, can we read a personal
wish, a personal ethos, into the poem? Can it be
that Pope, crushed by the bleakness of the contingent salvation inferred from the philosophic and
cosmic optimism he systematically developed with
the assistance of Bolingbroke, might have wished
to go beyond mere submission, contentment, or
hope and to be comforted with the expectation of
eternal bliss, even at the cost of intellectual con-
sistency?[21] Sentimentally, therefore, he might

have cherished more of the attractive paradisiacal hope for man and himself than the frigidly abstract happiness in relative perfection man was supposed to feel in his fixed station on the chain of being. Whatever the reason, the result is that when "Hope . . . lengthen'd on to Faith" (IV, 341-43), Pope imparted an emotional movement to his religious testament in *An Essay on Man*. The evidence of this poem and his own life suggests that Pope did not allow his mind to be deformed by the intricacies of dogmatic theology. But by attempting to place his beliefs within the conceptual framework of Christianity, Pope complicated his interpretation of the order of God's Providence and confused his definition of the divine perfection that is "Right." That Pope himself was aware of the direction of this movement is indicated in his letter to a close friend, Caryll, 1 January 1733/34:

To the best of my judgment the author shews himself a Christian *at last* in the assertion, that all Earthly Happiness as well as Future Felicity depends upon the doctrine of the gospel, love of God and man, and that the whole aim of our being is to attain happiness here, and hereafter by the practice of universal charity to man, and entire resignation to God. More particular than this he could not be with any regard to the subject, or manner in which he treated it.[22]

NOTES: I

1. "Letters or Essays Addressed to Alexander Pope: The Introduction," *The Works of Henry St. John, Lord Viscount Bolingbroke* (London, 1754), III, 314.
2. *Ibid., Works,* III, 329.
3. All references to *An Essay on Man* are to the Twickenham edition by Maynard Mack (New Haven: Yale University Press, 1951), Vol. III, Pt. i.
4. For a very good illustration of what Pope does *not* discuss, see Gilbert Burnet's *Exposition of the XXXIX Articles of the Church of England* (1699). I refer to the fourth edition, 1787. Burnet, for example, makes a clear distinction between natural and revealed religion at the very beginning of his commentary on the first and fundamental article of the Church of England confession, "Of Faith in the Holy Trinity": "The natural Order of things required, That the First of all Articles in religion should be concerning the Being and Attributes of God: For all other Doctrines arise out of this. But the Title appropriates this to the Holy Trinity; because that is the only part of the Article which peculiarly belongs to the Christian Religion; since the rest is Founded on the Principle of Natural Religion." (p. 17)
5. Joseph Spence, *Anecdotes,* ed. S. W. Singer (London, 1820), p. 315.
6. Bolingbroke, *Works,* III, 325.
7. Shaftesbury, *Characteristics, An Inquiry Con-*

cerning Virtue or Merit, I, iii, 3: " . . . in another
hypothesis (that of perfect theism) it is under-
stood 'that whatever the order the world produces, is in the main both just and good.' Therefore in the course of things in this world, whatever hardship of events may seem to force from
any rational creature a hard censure of his private condition or lot, he may by reflection never-
theless come to have patience, and to acquiesce
in it." [Ed. J. M. Robertson (London: Richards,
190), I, 278.]

8. *Essay on Man,* ed. M. Mack (Roxburgh Club
   Edn., 1962), Epistle I, folio 6. See also Twickenham edn., p. xxiv, n. 1.

9. Mack cites four letters by Pope that illustrate
   his use of the expression "Whatever is, is right":
   to Caryll, 3 September 1718; to Martha Blount,
   1715 or 1727; to Swift, 20 April 1733; to the Earl
   of Orrery, 10 December 1740. One more may be
   added to this list: to Swift, 19 December 1734.
   Mack refers to the Elwin-Courthope edition of
   Pope's letters. In this essay I refer to *The Correspondence of Alexander Pope,* ed. George Sherburn
   (Oxford: Clarendon, 1956). For the letters noted
   above, see I, 499, 319; III, 365, 444-45; IV, 304.

10. *Cf.* William Warburton, *A Vindication of Pope's
    Essay on Man* (London, 1740), p. 99.

11. *Cf.* Warburton, *Vindication,* pp. 18, 19, 27.

12. *Cf.* Burnet, *Exposition,* p. 32: "Which way soever
    God governs the World, and what Influence so-
    ever he has over Men's Minds, we are sure that the

governing and preserving his own Workmanship
is so plainly a Perfection, that it must belong to a
Being infinitely perfect: And there is such a
Chain in Things, those of the greatest consequence arising often from small and inconsider-
able ones, that we cannot imagine a Providence,
unless we believe everything to be within its Care
and View." In his *Dictionary* (1755), Samuel
Johnson defines Providence (2) as "The care of
God over created beings; divine superintendence."

13. Jean Pierre de Crousaz, *A Commentary on Mr.
Pope's Principles of Morality, or Essay on Man*
(London: Cave, 1742), pp. 52, 54, 80. This is
Samuel Johnson's translation. Swift, incidentally,
in a letter to Pope, 1 May 1733, ascribes, as he puts
it, the expression "What is, is best" to "the
thought of Socrates in Plato, because it is permitted or done by God. I have retained it after
reading Plato many years ago." Pope himself
attributes it to Socrates in the letter to Orrery,
10 December 1740, cited in note 9 above. See
Correspondence, IV, 304; and V, 11-12.

14. In a letter to Louis Racine, 1 September 1742,
Pope disavows the fatalism of Leibnitz. See *Correspondence*, IV, 416.

15. Bless: III, 111, 310.
Blessed, Bless'd, Blest: I, 75, 96, 125, 188, 286;
II, 148, 270; III, 66, 79, 255, 300; IV, 87, 96, 142,
147, 314, 317, 324, 351, 371.
Blesses: III, 300.
Blessing: I, 94, 189; III, 62, 212; IV, 39, 62, 96,

139, 269, 354.

Bliss: I, 93, 189, 282; III, 81, 110; IV, 21, 58, 94, 301, 311, 327, 335, 344, 346 (2), 350, 360, 397.

In his *Dictionary*, Johnson defines "To Bless" as "To make happy; to prosper"; "Blessed" as "enjoying heavenly felicity"; "Blessing" as "(1) Benediction; a prayer by which happiness is implored for anyone; . . . (4) Divine favour"; "Bliss" as (1) The highest degree of happiness; blessedness; felicity; generally used of the happiness of blessed souls."

16. In view of what he actually has written in the first epistle, Pope's remark to his friend Spence concerning his intention in the *Essay* is not quite candid: "Some wonder why I did not take in the fall of man in my Essay; and others how the immortality of the soul came to be omitted. The reason is plain: they both lay out of my subject, which was only to consider man as he is; in his present state, not in his past or future." [Spence, *Anecdotes*, p. 272.] The same can be said about his letter to Caryll, 8 March 1732/3, in which he defends himself against those who detected heresy in the poem: "Nothing is so plain as that he quits his proper subject, *this present world*, to insert his belief of *a future state*." [*Correspondence*, III, 354.] However, Pope in this letter may be referring to his remarks in the last epistle, as we shall soon see. In another letter to Caryll, 1 January 1733/4, Pope again defends the Christianity of the *Essay on Man* and specifically points

to his argument in the fourth epistle for "Future
Felicity . . . hereafter." [*Correspondence*, III,
400.] The full quotation is given at the very end
of this chapter.

17. *Cf.* Bolingbroke, *Works*, V, 65-66: "He, who acts
in a conformity to the nature of things, carries on
the system of God, and cooperates with him: and
surely to put the system of divine wisdom in exe-
cution, and to cooperate with the creator, is
honor enough for the creature. Thus we may
attain to the perfection of our nature, and, by pretending to no more, we may do it real honor:
whereas, by assuming that we imitate God, we give
the strongest proof of the imperfection of our
nature, whilst we neglect the real, and aspire
vainly at a mock honor; as pride, seduced by
adulation, is prone to do; and as religious pride,
wrought up by self-conceit into enthusiasm, does
above all others." See also a letter by Bolingbroke
to Swift, 2 August 1731, in which he argues in the
context of the *Essay on Man* against the idea of
a future state of rewards and punishments. [*Correspondence*, III, 213-14.] It is interesting to see
that Archbishop William King, who is said to
have had some influence on Pope, likewise argues
against a special immortality for mankind. See
his *Essay on the Origin of Evil* (London, 1731),
pp. 143-44.

18. Bolingbroke, *Works*, V, 337-38, 341, 390-92. See
also, for other statements that are similar to
Pope's in V, 377, 384, 489, 493. The last quota-

tion parallels the remark made by Pope to Swift, 20 April 1733, about Gay's death: "I now as vehemently wish, you and I might walk into the grave together, by as slow steps as you please, but contentedly and cheerfully: Whether that ever can be, or in what country, I know no more, than into what country we shall walk out of the grave. But it suffices me to know it will be exactly what region or state our Maker appoints, and that whatever Is, is Right." [*Correspondence*, III, 365.] In this respect, Warburton's interpretation of the *Essay* is incorrect. Pope shows how happiness and unhappiness "fall indifferently here on earth to good and bad," Warburton declares in his attempt to make the theology of the *Essay* palatable to the orthodox, "and from thence brings an admirable Argument for a future state." [*Vindication*, p. 3.] Pope does nothing of the sort.

19. See I *Tim.*, i, 5: "For the end of the Commandment is love out of a pure heart"; and *Col.*, iii, 14: "love which is the bond of perfectness." Also *Titus*, ii, 2.

20. Thus Pope anticipates a remark made during his last illness, 19-29 May 1744: "I am so certain of the truth of the Soul's being immortal, that I seem to feel it within me, as it were by Intuition." [*Correspondence*, IV, 526.] But this hope expressed near death differs from that expressed to Martha Blount many years before he began the *Essay on Man*: "The separation of my soul and body is what I could think of with less pain; for

I am very sure he that made it will take care of it, and in whatever state he pleases it shall be, that state must be right." [*Correspondence*, I, 319.] (Sherburn suggests the year 1715 for this letter to Miss Blount; Elwin-Courthope offer the year 1727. The language and the thought appear to support a later date, one close to the time he was writing the *Essay on Man.)* Obviously, as these letters demonstrate, Pope was simply uncertain about what to think concerning the hereafter.

21. See, for example, his conventional consolation addressed to the new Earl of Oxford on the death of his infant son, 7 November 1725: "Our comfort is certainly Beyond this world, because the Best of men have none here, under those very misfortunes which most affect them." [*Correspondence*, II, 337.]

22. *Correspondence*, III, 400. My italics.

II

THE CONVERSATION AND THE FRAME OF LOVE: IMAGES OF UNITY

*"As the small pebble stirs
the peaceful lake. . . ."*

AN ESSAY ON MAN, IV, 364

We shall start our discussion of the use of which Pope puts some imagery in *An Essay on Man* with Samuel Johnson's remarks: "Pope may have had from Bolingbroke the philosophick *stamina* of his *Essay* . . . We are sure that the poetical imagery, which makes a great part of the poem, was Pope's own."[1] "The subject is perhaps not very proper for poetry," Johnson says elsewhere. But he is willing to admit, however grudgingly, that it possesses a "dazzling splendour of imagery" which, he adds harshly, disguises "penury of knowledge and vulgarity of sentiment."[2] With only some of these views, of course, would Bolingbroke have concurred. He himself reminded the author that he should not write as a philosopher but as a poet: "The business of the philosopher is to dilate, if I may borrow this word from Tully, to press, to prove, to convince; and that of the poet to hint, to touch his subject with short and spirited strokes, to warm the affections, and to speak to the heart."[3]

Not that Pope needed reminding, for as a practicing poet he could well appreciate the difficulty of his problem—how to make passionate poetry out of cold philosophy. In "The Design" prefixed to the *Essay*, Pope writes in his typically lively and lucid manner about this problem. Unable to be only abstract even in prose, he must provide a kind of vivid

37

immediacy for his ideas by means of a concrete
imagery. Thus in the prose introduction he develops two images to communicate his intention: a
learned physiological simile, the anatomy of the
body and mind (p. 7, lines 12-16),[4] and a navigation
figure (p. 7, lines 20-21), one to which he returns
and elaborates in detail at the end of the introduction (p. 8, lines 10-19) as well as at the end of the
poem (IV, 380-6), where it serves quietly and
neatly to round out the thought, a voyage into
the sea of philosophy successfully concluded with
the help and guidance of Bolingbroke.[5]

As the words in "The Design" indicate, Pope was
highly conscious of his problem — to render abstract philosophy into concrete poetry. He states
that he chose verse and rhyme rather than prose to
give vividness and strength to the expression, to aid
memory, and to be concise, forceful and graceful.
He sums up his views on this critical problem as
follows: "I was unable to treat this part of my subject more in detail, without becoming dry and tedious; or more *poetically* without sacrificing perspicuity to ornament, without wandring [*sic*] from the
precision, or breaking the chain of reasoning" (p.
8). From this remark some readers may infer that
Pope appears to think of the figures used in poetry
to be merely ornamental but not functional or
organic. However, this is not what he really means.
The context makes clear that it is the excessive

elaboration of figures and conceits to which he objects; such cannot contribute to clarity and exactness. Certainly, in view of his own practice, Pope did not mean that *all* figures should be excluded from poetry. The fact is that he used figures to communicate his ideas more lucidly and precisely, to strengthen the reasoning, and to create poetry. The correct interpretation, then, must be that excess in figure ought to be checked, for it obscures the thought. The poet must keep his eye on his argument and, in accordance with the principles of propriety and decorum, choose only that imagery which would clarify and enliven the thought. This does not mean that Pope always succeeded in rendering the thought of the four epistles in poetry. He himself modestly confesses to failure and hopes that his other ethical works (the *Moral Essays)* "will be less dry, and more susceptible to poetical ornament."[6]

Our critical problem is thus set up: Does Pope indeed use images in his *Essay on Man* ornamentally, decorating the poem with casually selected images, or functionally and organically, thereby achieving coherence and synthesis through a careful selection and deliberate development of a pattern of imagery?[7]

[i]

Two large focal images unite the four epistles of Pope's *Essay on Man*. The first is dramatic, an

image of conversation. This provides the rhetorical
framework and is the best sustained image of the
whole work. The second is static, an image of nature
conceived of as a vast frame that comprehends, in
ever-decreasing circles, spheres, wheels, or orbits,
the world, society, and individual, man on a point
or station, and next to nothing. This second image
complex expresses the philosophic theme.

With regard to the first, we are asked to imagine
at the beginning of the *Essay* a serious dialogue
between the author Pope and his friend Henry St.
John, Viscount Bolingbroke. ("Let us. . . expati-
ate"; "let us beat, . . . try, . . . explore, . . . Eye,
. . . shoot, . . . And catch, . . . and Laugh where we
must . . . " I, 1-15). This conversation, suggested by
the use of the first person plural, then shades im-
perceptibly into the sustained image of Pope the
instructor expounding (undoubtedly in Bolingbroke's presence) God and His mysterious ways to
his unhappy complaining pupil ("thy," "thee": I,
31-4).[8] Sometimes the pupil is identified with ge-
neric man, whose complaints provide the loquaci-
ous mentor with the topics of his discourse: "Presumptuous Man" (I, 35); "Go, wond'rous creature"
(II, 19); "Remember, Man" (IV, 35) — or is alle-
gorically pictured as an abstract personification,
"Pride" (I, 132), whereby Pope is enabled to comment obliquely on man's foolish objections to God's
perfect system. But generally through the four epis-

tles, Pope addresses his implied pupil, using the second person or the imperative and thereby making clear the direction of his remarks.

In the first epistle, to show how Pope makes the dramatic situation clear, a few examples may be cited: "say not" (69), "Say rather" (70), "thy riot" (81), "thy Reason" (82), "Hope humbly" (91), "Wait . . . adore" (92), "Go, wiser thou!" (113), "Cease, then" (281), "Know thy" (283). In the second, examples running from the very beginning to the very end again underline the dramatic image: "Know . . . thyself" (1), "Trace Science" (43), "Then see" (51) — followed by a long lecture on psychology — "Ask your own heart" (215), "See" (267, 271), "Behold" (275), "thine" (292), "See! and confess" (293). This method continues in the third epistle: "Look round, . . . behold" (7), "See" (9, 13, 15, 16), "thou fool" (27), "Thou too" (70), "Know" (80), "Nor think" (147), "See" (169) — and then Pope discourses through Nature personified (171-98), followed by a long impersonal lecture on the origin of society that reaches the end of the epistle. In the fourth, however, Pope returns to Bolingbroke, whom he has almost forgotten (18, 260, 373-74), and so gives the impression that his agreeable companion is still present. But his attention is as before chiefly focused on Man, his foolish pupil: "Know" (77), "you go by" (128), "Act well" (194), "Look next" (217), "you hear" (239),

"Bring then" (269), "Know then" (309), "Gives
thee" (354). Occasionally in this epistle, the dis-
puting pupil is permitted utterance (149, 158, 160,
199). Finally, the admonitory lecture on virtue and
benevolence is polished off with a personal invoca-
tion to his own teacher, Bolingbroke, and so Pope
returns to the initial situation in the beginning of
the first epistle and gives a sense of dramatic unity
to the whole essay.

As for the character of the pupil, because he
merges so often with abstract man, the subject of
the *Essay*, the impression is given that he is a rep-
resentative and indistinct figure, a stereotyped
mixture of good and evil, the rational and irrational.
However, Pope's scornful attitude suggests that
the pupil does have some individuality, albeit unpleasant. For Pope's compulsion to satire fixes on
the negative traits: thus, the pupil is pictured as
weak, blind, and short; foolish, proud, and dull; a
mere point; a rebel, a little less than angel who
would be more; a presumptuous scientist with a
misdirected intellect. Pope's antitheses also help us
see him as a mass of nearly paralyzing inconsistencies, a confused enigma to himself and his studi-
ous observer: a slave and a deity; imperial yet a
vile worm; charged by self-love and a ruling passion,
yet checked, but imperfectly, by reason; virtuous
yet vicious. But Pope is not entirely pessimistic and
does not always denigrate his pupil. So, especially

towards the conclusion, he is shown to be capable of the virtues of charity and sympathy, through which he can achieve real happiness and stability; and he is hopeful of eternal bliss in the immortal state, and apparently receptive to rational, non-fanatical proposals of natural religion.

In short, Pope's pupil is Everyman, and he should be seen as Swift (in his letter to Pope, September 29, 1725), saw man, perhaps Gulliver, as *rationis capax*, not *animal rationale* — a man only capable of reason, certainly not one with a purely rational soul, for his behavior is not always wise. And most of all, the assumption is made that the pupil, although not particularly bright, is not altogether dull and hopeless because, being such a patient and respectful listener, he ought to profit from his master's eloquent discourses and show some moral improvement.

We must conclude, then, that Pope consistently maintains a dramatic point of view throughout the four discourses of his *Essay*, modulating his tone as he would in a real-life situation as he moves from one character trait of his pupil and one argument to another: wry, comic, mocking, pathetic, disgustful, contemptuous, scornful, solemn, and exalted. Through a framing image of a three-way conversation he unifies his vision and makes more vivid and lively and human what would otherwise be an abstract, dry and tedious series of lectures.

[ii]

The second focal image is far more complicated
and subtle than the image of the dramatic conversation because, expressive of the basic ideological
theme of the *Essay*, it includes a wide diversity of
interrelated details. As in the *Essay on Criticism*,
Nature is the regulative principle in the *Essay on
Man;* and, as in the earlier poem, Pope presents a
distinct image of it, although it takes in all the objects in the universe created by God, and its very
comprehensiveness and complexity militate against
definition. But because it underlies the meaning
and message of the philosophic poem, Pope cannot
afford to be fuzzy and must define Nature clearly.
After obscuring details for the moment are brushed
aside, what emerges as the central integrating image
is an astronomical vision of Nature as a huge frame
originally constituted by God: a dynamic machine
shaped as a vast circle, the macrocosm or "gen'ral
frame" (I, 264), enfolding an infinite series of
smaller circles, including that of man, the micro-
cosm, upheld and kept secure by a chain, and finally
coming to rest on one point or at nothing.[9]

But at the very beginning of the first epistle,
Pope's view of Nature is representational rather
than diagrammatic. It is like the harmonious confusion of *Windsor Forest,* a complex order in variety. Neither a complete wilderness nor a wholly
cultivated garden, neither profuse nor chaotic, its

key is simply order, "plan" (I, 6). Divine like the archetypal Eden, yet it contains intimations of evil (I, 8). While in *Windsor Forest* the image of nature takes in Eden and is then extended to England, in the *Essay on Man* it widens to infinity, taking in all of creation, extending not only to man's moral life ("this scene of Man," I, 5) but the cosmos as well.[10]

It is by no means a static image. We must think of Pope as our urbane host, taking us out of the city and the court, where some people attempt to satisfy their petty ambition with "meaner things" (I, 1-2) than philosophy, and into the country for a breath of clean, fresh air. He makes us look around with him as he points to the variety of natural details in the landscape. He even imagines a lively hunting scene, for it is daytime (I, 5-14).[11] But then, after the hunt ceases at nightfall, we are forced to gaze up at the immense sky full of stars, and to sense the vastness of space (I, 17-31). Thus the image enlarges and elevates the soul.[12] Like our host, we are overwhelmed by the sublimity of the night scene and made to feel weak and little in the presence of divine infinity. We are thus literally made to come face to face with the naturalistic theme — man as but a puny part of a vast natural scene; and, almost before we are aware of it, the scientific image of the ordering mechanical frame emerges.

It begins to take shape first with the idea of man's "station" (I, 19), the astronomical point from which man may look up to the ordered immensity of interstellar space and a plurality of worlds (I, 21-34), a panoramic view that Pope soon sums up in the metaphor of the "frame"[13] constructed of "bearings,"[14] elastic springs or, perhaps, weight-supporting beams, and uniting "ties,"[15] knots or fastenings, and "strong connections" (I, 29-30).

The image of the frame that Pope is asking us to see is not so sharply outlined as we should like it to be. But we can clearly sense from his account a supporting structure, a fabricated contrivance enclosing something else, or an engine constructed of several parts, in accordance with the numerous contemporary definitions of the term. In eighteenth-century common usage, the word "frame" may suggest an image of a printing machine or even of a weaver's loom; but the words that appear to define its context in the *Essay*, such as "bearings," "ties," and "connections," derive from architecture. All the definitions provided by the contemporary dictionaries (documented in the footnotes) agree on the mechanical nature of the structure, whatever it may precisely refer to — the printer's, builder's, or weaver's trade; hence it may be that because Pope has all three in mind the image of "th'aethereal frame" (I, 270) is not blurred or ambiguous so much as it is comprehensive and all-inclusive —

which is as it should be for an astronomical metaphor. In his *Dictionary* (1755), Samuel Johnson
provides a good idea of the way in which Pope uses
this metaphor. He defines this word (n.s.) as "a
fabrick, anything constructed of various parts or
members." Other definitions are "mechanical con-
struction" and "anything made so as to inclose or
admit something else." In general, the idea that
Johnson stresses is that of an ordering contrivance,
as in the illustration that he takes from Hooker:
"If the *frame* of the heavenly arch should dissolve
itself, if celestial spheres should forget their wonted
motions, and by irregular volubility turn themselves
any way, as it might happen. . . . "

This cosmic frame is, to continue with this explanation of Pope's vision, perhaps suspended —
but, more exactly, supported or "upheld" by "the
great chain, that draws all to agree, And when
drawn supports . . . " (I, 33-4). That is, when the
chain is linked up and drawn tight, it pulls all loose
ends up, making them taut, regular, equal or even.[16]
At precisely this point, Pope may actually be imagining an enormous mechanical loom in which all the
loose ends of the strings are drawn tightly together
and made equal; or he may also be imagining an
enormous orrery, an elaborate mechanical representation of the solar system made up of discs
and spheres designed to illustrate the motions of
the planets and moons.[17] As the context is spe-

cifically astronomical, it suggests that the verb
"draw" carries a connotation of "pull" or "tension"
as in "attraction," thereby referring to Newton's
new theory of magnetism or gravitation, which, as
Pope later explains (III, 9-12), "Form'd and
impell'd" "The single atoms" and segments of the
material world "to embrace." Thus this tight but
invisible chain, Pope says towards the end of the
fourth epistle, "links th'immense design, Joins
heav'n and earth, and mortal and divine" (IV, 333-
34).

In fine, the total image of the frame is that of a
mechanical design or contrivance, a supporting
structure perhaps like a huge loom or orrery, upheld by a tightly drawn chain, the parts of the chain
operating on the principle of attraction which draws
the individual links or units together. This frame
is "gen'ral," Pope states at the conclusion of the
first discourse (I, 264), constituting the universe
of nature — God's stable, perfect, and finished universe; sanctified by God, it is expressive of a divinely established "eternal Order," "God framed a
Whole, the Whole to bless," with "creature link'd
to creature, man to man" (III, 111-14). Thus the
argument from design, which underlies Pope's argument, begins, proceeds through, and ends in this
complex image: "Account for moral, as for nat'ral
things" (I, 162). That is to say, the problem of evil
can be explained by referring to the whole unified

and neatly connected, or linked-up, frame of nature, its variety and plenitude, and its general operational laws which justify any apparent inconsistencies of imperfections:

> *The gen'ral Order, since the Whole began,*
> *Is kept in Nature, and is kept in Man.*
> (I, 171-72)

The image can be applied to the human frame (II, 130, 137).[18] And elsewhere, at the conclusion of the third epistle, after describing the orderly double motions of the planets in the whole solar system (III, 313-6), Pope sums up by identifying divine and natural forces and picturing the proper posture of man in society through an image of a frame with parts linked together (III, 317-8):[19]

> *Thus God and Nature link'd [the parts of]*
>   *the gen'ral frame,*
> *And bade Self-Love and Social be the same.*

We have yet to indicate the precise shape of the divine and immutable frame of nature which Pope had so succinctly and cryptically described in I, 29-34. In a simile which fills in the details, Pope envisages it as a complicated mechanism with countless moving parts, a vast human works comprising bearings or elastic springs and wheels, circles within circles, as in the image of the movements of

a clock (I, 53-9). This image provides a clear clue.
Indeed, the idea of the circle appears so often in
connection with natural phenomena, Pope using
such words as "wheel," "sphere," "roll," "bubble,"
"world," as well as "circle" itself, that the reader
cannot help inferring that such must be the shape
of the central image: the frame as a tautly drawn
circle.[20]

Thus, for example, to realize the view of the circular frame, Pope pictures a plurality of worlds in
which "planets circle other suns" (I, 26). As noted
before, he sees man's position in the whole universal scheme of things as part of some vast clockworks
where man fulfills one small function or movement
among "A thousand movements" (I, 54) and "acts
second to some sphere unknown" and "Touches
some wheel" (I, 58-9). He also sees man as merely
"a point" in "space," yet "perfect in a certain
sphere" (I, 72-3). Understanding of such perfection,
however, is not granted to the parts that constitute
the whole: so man is blind, like the gentle lamb
doomed to slaughter, yet his blindness and that of
all finite created beings is a natural endowment,
"kindly giv'n," Pope declares in astronomical terms,
"That each may fill the circle mark'd by Heav'n" (I,
85-6). In God's eye, all is equal: the destruction of
the great and the tiny has equal significance —
sparrow or hero, atoms or systems, "And now a
bubble burst, and now a world" (I, 89-90) — the

circular shape of the tiny bubble being paralleled (through simultaneous balance and antithesis) by the circular shape of the immense world.[21]

Furthermore, Pope states emphatically, should "All" through rebellious pride "quit their sphere, and rush into the skies" (I, 123-4), they but "invert the laws of Order," and sin "against th'Eternal Cause" (I, 129-30). Therefore, to prevent such exorbitation, man should submit to the limitations of the senses which correspond to his species; only angels, belonging to a superior species, can properly hear "the music of the spheres" (I, 202). And every subordinate circle must contribute to the fullness of the whole creation — "each system in gradation roll, Alike essential to th'amazing Whole" (I, 247-8). Here the complicated series of circles, of wheels within wheels, merges suggestively with the natural garden image that begins the work, as Pope glances back to "A mighty maze" (I, 6).[22] Let there be but the slightest break or imperfection in any system, Pope continues, the divine circle of order and coherence will be broken, and things will go awry (I, 250-57):[23]

> ... *the Whole must fall.*
> *Let Earth unbalanc'd from her* orbit *fly,*
> *Planets and Suns run lawless thro' the sky,*
> *Let ruling Angels from their* spheres *be hurl'd,*
> *Being on being wreck'd, and* world *and* world,

Heav'n's whole foundations to their centre *nod,*
And Nature trembles up to the throne of God:
All this dread Order break — for whom? . . .

Pope concludes his first discourse by declaring that it is impious for man to rebel against the divine dispensation by attempting to move from his point in the great chain supporting the "gen'ral frame" or "aethereal frame" (I, 264, 270). Man must "Submit" (I, 285) to God's overall plan for him, being but a subordinate part of "one stupendous Whole" (I, 267). Man must "Know" his "own point" (I, 283), his special position in the celestial sphere (as in I, 72, "point" in "space"), or in the spatial and spiritual scheme of things, and accept whatever "blindness" or "weakness" with which he happens to be endowed by the creation.[24] For no matter what circle man may inhabit, he is sure to be "as blest" as he ought or as he deserves to be, according to his place in the larger system of things: "In this, or any other sphere, Secure to be as blest as thou canst bear" (I, 285-6).

In the second discourse, Pope continues to see man framed by a circle. But his vision is colored by irony and contempt. In his satire on the impious pride of man now become an astronomer, he pictures the presumptuous scientist foolishly trying to "mount" (II, 19) the celestial spheres — where he ought not to be, getting dizzy and falling. This astronomer presumes to "Instruct the planets in what orbs to run" (II, 21), and to "soar with Plato to th'empyreal sphere" (II, 24). Mystical inspiration, like that of the Plotinian followers of Plato, permits him to "tread the mazy round" (II, 25) where, losing good sense, he thinks he imitates God. But like Eastern priests who worship the sun, he really runs "in giddy circles" (II, 27). The mental effort of the proud scientist to mount the sphere of "Eternal Wisdom," to which Pope says he does not naturally belong, is patently absurd: "Then drop into thyself, and be a fool!" (II, 29-30). We must image the scientist dropping down through the astronomical spheres to the level and station appropriate to a humble human being.

Pope's image of the divine universal order as a circular frame is repeated at the conclusion of the third epistle, where the image is applied to the hierarchical structure of society. Here Pope describes the "World's great harmony that springs From Order, Union" (III, 295-6), a connection, that is, reconciling the opposing but necessary levels of the chain of being, "small and great, . . . weak and mighty," as it includes "Beast, Man, or Angel, Servant, Lord, or King" (III, 302). These parts of the social chain of living beings are, he envisions, drawn "to one point" and brought "to one centre" (III, 301), thereby implying (after what he has already written in the first epistle) a circle image.[25]

We may think of a series of circles enfolding one
another and drawing, as it were in perspective, to a
point. This inference of what was in Pope's eye is
confirmed by the following comparison of the motions of man's soul with the double circular motions
of the planets around the sun and on their own
axes (III, 313-5).

We may now diagram the focal image of the
poem: a circular frame enclosing an infinite series
of ever-decreasing circles and coming to a point.
God is the Whole Frame of Nature, and He "embraces" all the subordinate parts: "God loves from
Whole to Parts" (IV, 361). His will operates eter-
nally in "plastic Nature" (III, 9), according to the
principle of order suggested by the compact frame,
through the Chain of Being and Love. That is to
say, the links of this chain, themselves held together by attraction, bind or embrace all the subordinate strata in a descending scale of created
beings and things and hold the graded contents of
the frame taut (I, 33-4). Thus all the parts in the
scale are necessary: "nothing stands alone" (III,
25), for all must be connected and contribute to
the coherence of the whole. "The chain holds on,
and where it ends, unknown" (III, 26), Pope declares, infinity being at one end and "Nothing" at
the other (I, 240-1). Could we peer down from
God's position somewhere in infinity, we might see
the lines of the decreasing spheres or circles coming

to a point near Self-Love and Nothing, thereby suggesting an image of an inverted circular cone. This cone, should we think of it as if it were standing on a point, is symbolic of the precarious balance of the frame held together by just the right amount of tension in the magnetic chain. It appears, at least according to the emphasis given it by Pope, that much depends on man's ability to curb his pride as to whether the supporting chain will be broken, and, consequently, the frame topple over and collapse, or remain intact so that the frame will remain balanced and secure.

Traditionally, the circle symbolizes harmony (symmetry, proportion) and endlessness (eternity, infinity), and so it has come to stand for God, perfection, order (permanence, stability). It may even, as a bubble, symbolize life, round but fragile, evanescent.[26] Pope uses all these traditional meanings, including that of the bubble. And in the *Essay*, the circular frame, enfolding a series of circles like a "human works" such as an elaborate clock constructed of wheels within wheels and bearings or springs to control their movements, is by no means a forbiddingly frigid diagram, the complaint registered by Leslie Stephen.[27] As the image of the regulative principle of order and coherence, it serves as the governing metaphor of the whole poem and thereby contributes to the *Essay's* imaginative unity and the clarity of Pope's moral vision. Filled

in with the relevant naturalistic details permitted
in the chain of being, it became for the poet a
source of ecstatic mystery and wonder (I, 267-8):

> . . . *one stupendous Whole,*
> *Whose body Nature is, and God the soul.*

Here in this metaphor (as the soul is to the body,
so God is to nature) we may even detect an echo
of Newton's famous definition of infinite space as
the Sensorium of the Godhead.[28]

For Pope, moreover, this visual metaphor is endowed with profound meaning and emotion as he
poignantly describes man's difficult, perhaps in-
superable, task — how to find his proper point or
position in the vast frame, the fullness thereof comprehending all of nature and God: "That each
may fill the circle mark'd by Heav'n . . . " (I, 86).
For him, thus, the circle is definitely not broken.[29]
It is still in the early eighteenth century a significant emblem of unity, perfection, endlessness and
eternity, the emblem of the poet's faith, although
conceived in Newtonian and mechanical terms.

Indeed, the symbolic circle of perfection has such
deep meaning for Pope that he has also employed
it for the climax of the *Essay.* There (IV, 361-72)
as he emphasizes the expanding nature of man's
sympathy which "Grasp(s)" or embraces "the
whole worlds of Reason, Life, and Sense, In one

close system of Benevolence" (IV, 357-8), he experiences a beatific vision of ever-widening circles of altruism. This theme he symbolizes naturalistically by a "small pebble" stirring the water of a peaceful lake and producing wave upon wave of concentric circles. So the individual human soul, "mov'd" or "wake(d)" by self-love at its "centre,"[30] Pope says, can be benevolent and virtuous—it will encircle and "embrace" the people around, "Friend, parent, neighbour," then "country" and "human race," until almost at the extremities of the last enfolding circle—"Wide and more wide"—the circular waves or "o'erflowings of the sympathetic and virtuous mind" will include all living things in nature, "Take ev'ry creature in, of ev'ry kind," so that eventually earth, now an image of perfection, a full circle, will become a paradise and mirror heaven.[31] Thus as a simple representational image of nature becomes a profoundly moving symbol, Pope is enabled to resolve all those conflicts central to the condition of man and nature and to close his essay on a note of affirmation. In a rhetorical sense, then, Pope comes full circle, for the infinite benevolence that he requires of man in the last part of the last discourse is the same that he hopes of God in the first discourse.[32]

[iii]

It is difficult, and perhaps incorrect, to reduce the diversity of imagery of a work of the magnitude of

An Essay on Man to a single and simple formula.
Yet upon analysis we do see a structure of meaning
emerge. The poem yields enough evidence to demonstrate an imaginative figurative unity. A framing image of conversation is sustained throughout
the poem, providing a dramatic unity that animates
and humanizes, thereby making the ethical theme
vivid. Nor should the unobtrusive but framing
image of navigation be forgotten ("The Design,"
p. 7, lines 20-21; p. 8, lines 10-19; and IV, 379-86)
as a source of unity. But the central conceptual
image—one that best illuminates the writer's meaning and most completely harmonizes the apparent
chaos of thought and natural phenomena—is a circular mechanical frame drawn tightly together by
the gravitational forces of the sacred chain of being
and love. This image is first used to express the
original constitution of Nature according to God
and the contemporary Newtonian astronomy; and
then it is extended to man and to society, carrying
with it all its scientific overtones. Thus as it figures
through the work and ties the discourses neatly together, this recurring image validates the propositions set forth; reinforces the theme of unity, connection, and design; and, finally, provides organic
and imaginative coherence. This frame shaped as a
taut circle is the poet's emblem of the ultimate order
and perfection of Nature to which man should
aspire, the embrace and the infinite love of God.

NOTES: II

1. *Boswell's Life of Johnson*, ed. G. B. Hill and L. F. Powell (Oxford, 1934-50), III, 403-4. In his *Life of Pope*, Johnson reiterated this idea: "The *Essay* plainly appears the fabrick of a poet: what Bolingbroke supplied could be only the first principles; the order, illustration, and embellishments must all be Pope's." [*Lives of the Poets*, ed. G. B. Hill (Oxford, 1905), III, 163.]

2. *Lives of the Poets*, III, 242, 243.

3. *Works of Henry St. John*, ed. David Mallet (1754), III, 317-18; R. W. Rogers, *The Major Satires of Alexander Pope* (Urbana: University of Illinois, 1955), p. 51.

4. The text is the Twickenham Edition by Maynard Mack (New Haven: Yale University Press, 1951), Vol. III, Part i.

5. When he was at work on the poem, Pope, in a comment to Spence (May, 1730), again expressed his overall intention in a navigation metaphor: "The first epistle is to be to the whole work, what a scale is to a book of maps; and in this, I reckon, lies my greatest difficulty: not only in settling and ranging the parts of it aright, but in making them agreeable enough to be read with pleasure." Joseph Spence, *Anecdotes*, ed. S. W. Singer (London, 1820), p. 16.

6. On the basis of his remarks in "The Design," it would be unfair to accuse Pope of conceiving that the function of imagery be superficially decorative. So J. M. Cameron, fixing upon the in-

adequacy of Pope's critical attitude, literally but
anachronistically takes him at his own word
and calls the *Essay on Man* "a poor philosophical
essay embellished with rhymes and other orna-
ments." ["Doctrinal to an Age," *Dublin Rev.*,
CCXXV (1951, Second Qtr), 55, 66-7.] The most
we can say is that Pope's conscious intention and
awareness of the function of figure and image, as
he twice uses the word *ornament*, are inadequate
for an explanation of the function of rhetoric in
poetry, his own poetry included. Admittedly,
Pope's brief and simple observation clearly does
not do justice to the actual complexity of his
work. For Pope did not have the good fortune to
live after Coleridge, the father of critical organ-
icism, and to understand the complex contribu-
tions of the New Critics. Thus his rhetorical
theory, lacking this concept, lagged behind his
practice.

7. For example, Frederick S. Troy ["Pope's Images
    of Man," *Massachusetts Rev.* I (Winter, 1960),
    375] denies that Pope uses recurring images in
    the *Essay on Man*.

8. Thomas Edwards detects humor in the opening
    lines of Epistle I. He says that the joke is that
    Pope is instructing the lecturing Bolingbroke, not
    the other way around. [*This Dark Estate* (Berke-
    ley: University of California Press, 1963).] But
    surely this cannot be true in view of Pope's re-
    spectful attitude to Bolingbroke expressed at the
    very end of the last epistle and elsewhere in

the poem.

9. For *frame* as a *machine*, a scientific commonplace in the literature of the sixteenth and seventeenth centuries, see John Arthos, *The Language of Natural Description in Eighteenth Century Poetry* (Ann Arbor: University of Michigan Press, 1949), pp. 176-180.

10. Warburton's allegorical interpretation of these naturalistic details is interesting: "The *wild* relates to the human *passions*, productive (as he explains it in the second epistle) both of good and evil. [Hence *weeds* = evil; *flowers* = good.] The *Garden*, to human *reason*, so often *tempting* us to transgress the bounds God has set to it, and wander in fruitless enquiries." [Note in Warburton's edition of *An Essay on Man* (1743), p. 2.] Wakefield takes exception to Warburton's note, which he calls "too far fetched and erroneous." His view follows: "Man, as a compound of Virtue and Vice, Wisdom, and Folly, may be compared to a *wild* of promiscuous weeds and flowers: or, as a being, perpetually liable to the seductions of passion and the allurements of worldly pleasures, may be considered as a *garden*, holding forth a solicitation of his appetite in the fruit of an interdicted tree." [Gilbert Wakefield, *Observations on Pope* (London, 1796), pp 154-55.]

11. Joseph Warton does not care for this image: " . . . these metaphors [in the opening lines], drawn from the field sports of setting and shooting, seem below the dignity of the subject, and an unnatural

mixture of the ludicrous and serious." He cites
lines 13 and 14 as especially bad. [*Essay . . . on
Pope* (1782), II, 124; also *Works of Alexander
Pope*, ed. Joseph Warton (London, 1797), III,
13.] Nor does Bowles favor the hunting metaphor.
He adds that the minuteness with which Pope
pursues the hunting figure gets him into trouble
when he writes of "eyeing a walk." [*Works of
Alexander Pope*, ed. W. L. Bowles (London,
1806), III, 14.] But we may ask why the poet
cannot *eye* a walk carefully (i.e., aim at it) for
anything that may appear. Wakefield believes
"This whole passage is one of the happiest speci-
mens of poetical dexterity in the conduct of an
illusion, without aberration or incongruity, that
has fallen under my observation." [*Observations
on Pope*, p. 155.] The image has been explicated
by J. L. Kirby, *The Explicator*, I (Nov., 1942),
12, who shows how the hunting figure develops
naturally from the image of an English garden.

12.   So Maynard Mack briefly says in his essay, "Wit
and Poetry and Pope: Some Observations on His
Imagery," *Pope and His Contemporaries*, ed. J.
L. Clifford (Oxford: Clarendon, 1949), p. 29.

13.   In the OED (III, 7, 8, 13) *Frame* is defined as
"A structure, fabric, or engine constructed of
parts fitted together . . . Applied to the heaven,
earth, etc. regarded as a structure." Nathanael
Bailey, *An Universal Etymological English
Dictionary* (London, 1728; 4th ed.) defines
A Frame as "a Figure, Form, Make: the Support-

ers of a Chain, Table, etc. The Outwork of a Clock, etc." *To Frame* he defines "to form, to create, to contrive, to build." The 1730 edition adds to the latter definition, "to fashion, to square." In his *Cyclopaedia* (1738, 2nd ed.), Ephraim Chambers defines *frame* in several different ways: "in joinery, etc. a kind of case, wherein a thing is set, or inclosed, or even supported; as a window frame, frame of a picture, of a table, etc." Also "a machine, used in divers arts," such as printing. Also "more particularly used for a sort of loom, whereon artizans stretch their linens, silks, stuffs, etc. to be embroidered, quilted, or the like." (For *Loom* Johnson has "the frame in which the weavers work their cloath," a definition that is derived from Bailey: "A Loom is the Frame a Weaver works upon or in.")

14. *Bearings* (OED, iii, 11): "springs, elastic spring." See also *Bear* sb[3]. This definition is a possibility which Pope himself does not neglect in his clockworks image that soon follows. But none of the eighteenth-century dictionaries consulted — Bailey, Chambers, Johnson — suggest it. Johnson's definition of *bearing* cannot apply to a loom. He refers to a builder's dictionary for an architectural definition and quotes from Pope's *Essay on Man*, I, 29, to illustrate this definition: "The site or place of anything with respect to something else." This is really Bailey's definition of *Bearing* according to its use in geography and navigation: " the situation of one place from an-

other." In his 1728 and 1730 editions, Bailey defines *Bearers* "[in Architecture]" as "Posts, or Brick Walls, which are trimmed up between the two Ends of a Piece of Timber to shorten its bearing"; and *Bearing* he defines "[in Carpentry]" as " the bearing of a Piece of Timber is the Space between the two fixed Ends of it, when it has no other support; which is called *bearing at length;* or between one End and a Post, Brickwall, etc. trimmed up between the Ends to shorten its bearing." This is Johnson's architectural definition. Chambers' source is the same as Bailey's.

15. In the OED, *ties* is defined simply as "that which anything is tied; a cord, band, or the like, used for fastening something; a knot, noose, or ligature." This is Johnson's definition: "knot, fastening." Bailey's definition of the verb *to Tie* (1730 and 1760 eds.) is the same: "to bind or join together by a knot"; and *to Tye* means simply "to bind." *Ties*, however, Bailey defines "[in a Ship] are those Ropes by which the Yards hang and that carry them up when the Halliards are strained." The OED also gives a definition of *tie* (9c) that refers to hand-loom weaving. The other words are not so ambiguous or obscure: "Strong connections, nice dependencies." Bailey: *nice* = "exact, curious, subtil"; *connections* = "a joining things together, a Dependency of one thing upon another"; *to Connect* = "to knit, join, or fasten together"; *Dependancy (sic)* = "a resting, stay-

ing, or relying upon; a Relation or Subjection to"; *to Depend*, "to hang on, to rely on, to proceed from." In his note to I, 29-31, Mack (Twickenham ed., pp. 16-7) believes that the key words signify a blended figure with architectural, hierarchical, and astronomical allusions. Another possibility we should like to suggest is that of a vast loom with pulleys that tie and draw the parts together.

16. See also III, 301-2, for "Draw" = pull "to one point," as in a cone or pyramid; and III, 317, "link'd" up "the gen'ral frame," for the image of the chain.

17. For a brief account of the orrery, see Michael Macklem, *The Anatomy of the World* (Minneapolis: University of Minnesota Press, 1958), pp. 53-5. The orrery was popular in the first half of the eighteenth century. But near the conclusion of the first part of his *Age of Reason* (1794), Thomas Paine also describes the orrery as a scale model of the universe: "It is a machinery of clockwork, representing the universe in miniature . . . ."

18. In his letters, Pope often makes this application, apparently a metaphorical commonplace. Some examples may be offered: "Your Head & your Limbs are of so good a Make, that the more Active the Machine is made to play, the better it workes: With such weak ones as mine, the least extraordinary Motion puts 'em out of frame. My Body agrees better therefore [*sic*] with Rest than Motion, my Mind with Conversation than Study"

(19 Aug. 1735); " . . . shaking my weak frame to pieces" (2 April 1738); "my weak frame being almost shook to pieces" (26 July 1739); "the Infirmity of my Frame" (2 August 1739); "my weak Frame" (13 Jan. 1742/3). [*The Correspondence of Alexander Pope*, ed. George Sherburn (Oxford: Clarendon, 1956), III, 483; IV, 92, 189, 190, 437.]

19. In a letter to the Earl of Orrery (10 Dec. 1740), Pope falls into an attitude that he adopted when writing the *Essay on Man* and metaphorically extends the meaning of the word "frame" to include human happiness. In this letter Pope is saying that God has united physical evil (such as death) and good so closely that human beings can scarcely be happy: "May every such Near, such Remoter Tye of Affection, be managed so gently by Providence, as to touch you with the soft, not gall you with the severe, Sensation; tho in the disposition of this System, God has been pleas'd (no doubt for good Ends, tho to us unseen) to unite them, too closely for the tender frame of *human* Happiness. Adieu my Lord; whatever *Is*, is *Right* . . . ." [*Corr.*, IV, 304.]

20. So Addison's vision of the astronomical "Shining Frame" is circular. See his famous ode on the creation in *Spectator 465* (23 August 1712). It should be noted that the word "verges" in this section (I, 59) means to *bend* or *turn*.

21. *Cf.* "bubbles" also in II, 288; III, 19-20.

22. *Cf.* "the mazy round" (II, 25) of the Plotinian fol-

lowers of Plato. Pope may have derived this figure from James Thomson who had in his *Winter* (1726) referred to "th'Eternal Scheme" as that "Mystic Maze." (lines 380-81)

23. My italics. Warburton's note for I, 251, explains the unbalanced earth as a reference to our planet falling out of orbit: "Being no longer kept within its orbit by the different directions of its progressive and attractive motions; which, like equal weights in a balance, keep it in an equilibre." *Cf.* I, 124.

24. The word "point" has clear astronomical overtones, referring to definite points of the celestial sphere, such as "point of heaven," a usage by Dryden. (See OED, 18, c.) Chambers' *Cyclopaedia* (ed. 1738), and Johnson's *Dictionary* (1755), definitions 9, 12, 13, bear out this opinion, too.

25. *Cf.* III, 14-5: "See Matter next, . . . Press to one centre still, the gen'ral Good."

26. Marjorie H. Nicolson, *The Breaking of the Circle* (Evanston: Northwestern University Press, 1950), p. 42.

27. Leslie Stephen, *History of English thought in the Eighteenth Century* (London: Smith, Elder, 2nd ed., 1881), II, 351. Recently, a similar criticism has been made by Thomas Edwards, *This Dark Estate*, pp. 42-5. Edwards believes that Pope's images of perfection are inferior to those of imperfection because they lack vividness and conviction. Pope is unable to treat "the whole" effec-

tively, Edwards says, because his vision of it is
mechanistic, static, foreign to human experience,
impossible to dramatize, vague and lacking in
natural particulars.

28. Newton, *Opticks*, III, i, Qu. 28; Marjorie H.
Nicolson, *Newton Demands the Muse* (Princeton:
University Press, 1946), pp. 104-5.

29. Contrary to what Professor Nicolson has written,
the metaphor of the circle had not disappeared
from English literature during the eighteenth
century. *(The Breaking of the Circle*, p. xxi.) It
is, as we have seen, clearly in Pope's *Essay on
Man*. To Pope, as to writers of the seventeenth
century and Plato in the *Timaeus*, it was equally
a circle of perfection, coherence, and order, even
though it includes the idea of infinity, the result
of the new astronomy. "The idea of infinity,"
Miss Nicolson declares (p. 145), "had utterly
demolished the Circle of Perfection." But the new
astronomy is assimilated into Pope's vision and
does not negate the idea of circular endlessness.
And it certainly is incorrect and inconsistent to
declare, in view of the symbolic meaning of endlessness that he gives to it, that "Pope's is the
closed circle, the circle of limitation." (p. 182)

30. This image should, of course, be related to Pope's
definition of virtuous happiness in IV, 311, as
"The only point where human bliss stands still."
As Gilbert Wakefield has said, "The allusion here
seems to be to the pole, or central point, of a
spherical body; which, during the rotatory mo-

tion of every other part, continues immoveable and at rest." [*Observations on Pope*, p. 195.] Thus it may be said that Pope sees the perfection of virtue in circular terms.

31. Owen Ruffhead has commented on the effectiveness of the pebble-in-the-water image: "Here we have another instance of the poet's happy choice of poetical embellishments. The simile he has employed, affords the clearest illustration of the expanding nature of benevolence, and establishes the truth of his reasoning, at the same time that it gives beauty to the poem." [*The Life of Alexander Pope* (London, 1769), p. 258.] The ever-widening circles in the water also appear in *The Temple of Fame*, 436-47, and for comical effects at the conclusion of *The Dunciad*, II, 405-10, and of IV, 605-18 (as a submerged metaphor). Edwin H. St. Vincent, *Aspects of Pope's Imagery* (Columbia University Unpublished Dissertation, 1962), pp. 30-1, 205-7, briefly comments on these circles.

32. The antitheses and their final resolution and synthesis also contribute to this concluding note of harmony and affirmation. But the functional role of antitheses is discussed in the following essay.

III

UNITY AND DIALECTIC:
THE STRUCTURAL ROLE
OF ANTITHESES

*"God and Nature
link'd the gen'ral frame."*

AN ESSAY ON MAN, III, 317

THE FIGURE of antithesis appears in such great numbers in Pope's *Essay on Man* (in round numbers totaling three hundred in 1285 lines, averaging about one to every four lines) that it may rightfully be considered the dominating figure of the whole work.[1] Again and again, Pope skillfully resorts to this rhetoric, the signature of his verse, to develop ideas with epigrammatic force and economy. The result is terse, pithy writing, characterized by density or fullness, the balance itself effecting a certain sharpness and polished clarity. When the balance is especially pronounced in numerous antitheses, the expression takes on a brittle and glittering quality. Undoubtedly, Pope refers to these stylistic effects of antitheses when, in "The Design" prefixed to the poem, he declares that he has chosen verse rather than prose because the brevity that it encourages in his expression permits him to make a more pungent and memorable instructive statement of his ethics: "much of the force as well as grace of arguments or instructions, depends on their conciseness" (p. 8). *Force, grace,* through *conciseness* — these clearly apply to the aesthetic effects of antitheses. But Pope goes even further than the creation of such stylistic effects. He also structures the thought of each of the epistles around large governing antitheses; and as he concludes the

thought of each by means of a dynamic synthesis
that reconciles these major conflicts, he is enabled
to sound a strong positive note of hope and affirmation. Such is the rhetorical pattern throughout the
Essay.

[i]

THE antithesis in the first epistle is the chief rhetorical device by means of which Pope presents his
major theme and at the same time controls and
orders the enormous diversity of the details of nature. In this epistle, there are about seventy antitheses for three hundred lines. But one large central antithesis, God and Man, governs all of them;
and this antithesis establishes the movement of this
epistle and directs it to an inevitable synthesis and
a feeling of rest. Often this fundamental opposition
is conceptualized as the Whole and Part (32, 60,
267), which, at the concluding synthesis, is equated
with "universal Good" and "partial Evil" (292).

God sees and controls the Whole, while Man can
see only the Part; such is Pope's contention. But,
Pope continues, despite his partial view, or perhaps
because of it, finite Man's opinion stubbornly op-
poses the infinite wisdom of God. In Pope's balanced rhetoric, this conflict is expressed more completely as follows: Man's opinion, uncertain and
erring because based only on a part of the evidence,
is that nature is characterized by chaos, chance,
and discord; but the opposing truth is that God's

wisdom has endowed the whole creation with perfect order, art, direction, and harmony. Further, Man also believes that he is favored (or ought to be) by nature's partial laws; but the truth is that God's Providence operates through nature's comprehensive and impartial laws (114-22, 146, 289-91) — a Providence that is "all good and wise Alike in what it gives and ... denies" (205-6).

To use one of Pope's illustrations, Man is as blind as the brute beasts, the horse and the ox, for they can neither see nor understand their ultimate direction (61-68). Let us examine this animal simile; it is a good example of the way in which Pope's imagination operates through finely balanced antitheses. At this point in his argument, Pope particularly wishes to emphasize Man's difficulty in his attempt at fathoming God's will. Man, that is to say, does not know the will of God that surely guides him, just as these beasts do not understand the will of Man that controls them. The horse, described as "proud" and "fiery" (61-62), is contrasted with the ox, "dull" (63), phlegmatic or stupid; so Man, too, in whom these opposing traits are synthesized, is characterized by "pride and dulness" (65). Further, Man "restrains" or "drives" (61-62) the horse which is, as we have already noticed, unaware of its goal; so Man himself is "check'd" or "impell'd (67) under similar uncertain conditions. On the other hand, the ox is at one time

treated as a sacrificial "victim" and at another wor-
shiped as a "God" (64); so Man does not know
what he is "doing" or why he is "suff'ring" (67);
and, moreover, he is like the ox, oppressed "this
hour" as "a slave," elevated "the next" to "a deity"
(68). This short paragraph, it is seen, is made coherent by a series of intricately balanced and opposed images of man and brute and by several
additional images that express contrasting attitudes
toward them — altogether seven in eight lines! The
result is a highly finished, densely carved cameo.

To Pope, the opposition between an infinitely
wise God who sees the Whole and blind Man who is
familiar only with a Part is fundamental because it
gives rise to Man's most poignant ethical problems
— how to conduct himself in accordance with divine will and with his assigned position in Nature's
plan (189-90); and how, when he knows he is imperfect, he can yet, paradoxically, find the measure
of his perfection: "say not Man's imperfect," Pope
writes; "Say, rather, Man's as perfect as he ought"
(69-70). Of course, it is difficult, if not impossible,
for Man, who by nature can see only a part, to
solve these moral problems as Pope sees them.
(And as a matter of fact, Pope never really does
provide a thoroughly convincing solution, for he is
compelled to resort to faith.) Nor is the difficulty
made easier by the presence of an internal conflict
that reflects rebellious Man's conflict with God.

That is, we may infer from Pope's satire and exhortations that Man is almost torn apart by two opposing forces — those rational and naturally instinctive forces that pressure him to "submit" humbly ("to reason right is to submit," 164, 285) to God's will and those irrational forces that egotistically urge him to nurse his rebellious pride, to attempt improvements upon the original creation, and to correct assumed evils and imperfections (35, 125, 161, 293). The famous series of antitheses that summarize Pope's view of Man in the beginning of the second epistle (II, 3-18) dramatizes this internal conflict and its enervating effects upon Man; and so, in conception, content, and spirit, they may be considered a part of the first epistle.[2]

Still, although Man's moral problems are perhaps impossibly difficult, Pope optimistically does hold out hope for their ultimate solution. But first, he insists that Man overcome his self-conflict; for only then can the major conflict between himself and God be resolved. At the conclusion of the first epistle Pope dramatizes this hopeful possibility in a synthesis. Man, he believes, can overcome his pride and can achieve understanding of his cosmic role simply through a recognition of the importance that the Part plays with respect to the Whole. This resolution he expresses in a mystical vision of unity, order, and perfection. It is as if in this vision God, who has designed the Whole, assimilates nonre-

sistant and subordinate parts, the "high" and "low,"
"great" and "small" (279). Thus each Part in this
assimilating vision must be perfect, according to
Pope's argument, for it serves a necessary and
essential function with respect to the orderly operations of the Whole: "Alike essential to th'amazing
whole" (247-50). Further, Pope argues, to clinch
the matter for ultimate good, each Part is really
perfect in itself because it partakes of the divine
spirit. God's "soul" informs and "equals all," and so,
because of His immanence, there can be no painful
antitheses, "no high, no low, no great, no small" to
disturb Man. Indeed, as Pope calls in additional
antitheses to help ("all" and "one," "body" and
"soul," "Nature" and "God"),

> All are but parts of one stupendous whole,
> Whose body Nature is, and God the soul.
>   (267-80)

Pope's solution, as we can see, is simply that of
orthodox religion, an act of faith. It certainly is not
unusual to believe that the immanence of God mag-
ically reconciles the contradictions in life and nature and transforms all conflict into harmony.

Once we understand how Pope's rhetorical method inevitably takes him toward the final harmony of
opposites, we can reread the introduction to the
poem and there sense anticipatory intimations of

this movement toward reconciliation. Almost every line and expression is ingeniously balanced in the opening paragraph (1-12), demonstrating how Pope's imagination operates compulsively in terms of sharply defined opposites. At first, Pope urges his friend Bolingbroke, to whom he is addressing the discourse, to "leave" ignoble matters, "meaner things, To low ambition and the pride of Kings" (1-2), that is, to low and high types of worldly ambition, and to dedicate himself to a study of noble philosophy. Then, in an explicit statement, Pope makes the assumption that underlies the argument of the epistle — that when a panoramic view of the Whole is taken, a view that includes all contradictions, nature and life will no longer appear to be a puzzling "maze," or labyrinth, but will be seen to have a clear "plan" (6) of order.

After making this fundamental assumption, Pope illustrates the major theme of the Whole and the Part with representational images of external nature whose antitheses symbolize the bewildering variety of all nature and life in which man must conduct himself, "this scene of Man" (5). "This scene," Pope's rhetoric makes definitely clear, comprises two contrasting parts — "A Wild," an uncultivated wilderness promiscuously scattered with "weeds," symbolizing evil, and "flow'rs," symbolizing good; and a "Garden," a cultivated plantation of trees heavy with "tempting . . . fruit" (7-8), symbolizing the problem of moral choice facing man in the world. Then, in the following three lines, Pope employs three antitheses, the images of which sum up the variety in the conditions of life and nature that man must study: "open" fields and "covert," or ground with sheltering vegetation (10); "latent tracts," the low places, plains and valleys, and "giddy heights," the high exposed places and mountains (11); and those beings that "blindly creep" on the ground and those that "sightless soar" through the air (12).[3] Pope here makes emphatic through repetition the lack of vision of those who can see only a part of nature. Clearly implied is the opposite, of course; indeed, it is Pope's positive message in the entire poem — that a satisfying vision comes only to those who do see, experience, and understand the whole panorama of nature and life, in the air *and* on the ground, on the high mountains *and* in the low valleys, in the open fields *and* in the sheltering trees and bushes.

Thus, in short, even in the very beginning of the work, Pope announces his theme in an antithesis, the opposition between God, the Whole, and Man, the Part. This major conceptual antithesis is resolved in a synthesis, described in a vision of order and design, or, to use Pope's word, of a "plan." Only those far-seeing visionaries who have deep enough insight into this plan can successfully reconcile apparent conflicts and inconsistencies, can, as Pope says, "vindicate," or explain,[4] "the ways of God to Man" (16).

Practically all of the subordinate data of observation in the first epistle illustrate the large comprehensive moral antitheses of the real goodness of the Whole as against the apparent evil of the Part, God's Providence against Man's Opinion, and, at the same time, they themselves are controlled by balanced antitheses. So Pope contrasts the "great" and the "small" (279) in the frame of nature: infinity and man (240), man and nothing (241), "Nature" and "Man" (172), "systems" and "atoms" (89), "world" and "bubble" (90), "Man" and "Fly" and "mite" (193-96), "earth" and "th'aethereal frame" (270), a planet and its "Satellites" (42), "oaks" and "weeds" (39-40). He also thinks of the objects in the great chain that constitutes all of nature as made up of "superior" and "inferior" beings and things, "above" and "below," or "upward" and "downward" (173-75, 235-36, 241-42): "Gods" and "Angels" (126), "God above" and "Man below" (17), "Man" and "Heav'n" (69), "aethereal Natures" and "human" nature (238), "angels" or "spirits" and "men" (79, 126), or "vile Man" and "rapt Seraph" (277-78), "men" and "brutes" (79), "hero" and "sparrow" (88). His view of the impartiality and timelessness of the laws of God and Nature is framed by further space and time antitheses: "soon or late," "here or there," "today" and "a

thousand years ago" (74, 75-76, 120). His view of
the scale of senses according to the great chain is
also presented in a series of "high" and "low" (279)
antitheses representing the extremes in sensitivity
in sight, smell, and hearing (209-16), and the extremes in behavior of the instinctive hog and the
"half-reas'ning elephant" (221-22). But he notes,
too, the difficulty of finding the dividing line in the
mind between such complex mental operations as
instinct and reason, remembrance and reflection,
thought and sensation (223-26). Lastly, when he
writes of the possibility of immortality in an eternal
hereafter as part of God's dispensation for the
Whole — "Man never Is, but always To be blest"
(96) [5] — Pope neatly and elaborately contrasts in
one paragraph the civilized, greedy Christian whose
"proud Science" teaches him to "stray" and lose
faith, with the "poor," humble savage "Indian" who,
lacking knowledge of astronomy, correctly follows
"simple Nature" and has faith in an impartial or
"equal" God (99-112).

In the first epistle, then, the antitheses are quite
apposite to Pope's theme of nature made up of
antagonistic differences: "All subsists by elemental
strife" (169). At the same time that they illustrate
this theme, they function in several ways to quicken
the movement of the ideas and to provide order,
coherence, and balance for the poet's vision of an
infinitely complex unity in variety. In this epistle,

the reconciliation of opposites in a comprehensive
synthesis sets a pattern of movement for contradictory ideas and states of being to which Pope
adheres in all the other parts of the poem. The
repetition significantly contributes to the rhetorical
unity of the whole work.

[ii]

THE antitheses in the second epistle continue un-
abated, announced by the ecstatic flurry of balanced
opposites dramatizing man's greatness and little-
ness, his ambiguity and confusion in the "middle
state" (3-18). After this introduction, two large
psychological antitheses, reason and passion or self-
love, and the conflict among the ruling passions
themselves, emerge and are shown to dominate the
movement of thought to an ultimate synthesis. The
usual subantitheses illustrate the major oppositions
or help carry the argument — a total in round numbers of seventy in three hundred lines. Images are
sometimes made to contrast with each other: fixed
plant-moving meteor, calm-storm, still frost-violent
tempest. Sometimes two opposing concepts are
juxtaposed in two words to form a paradoxical oxy-
moron: "darkly wise," "rudely great," " happy
frailties" (4, 241); or juxtaposed in one line: "the
rogue" who is "fair" or honest, the "fool" who is
"wise" (233), "one Man's weakness grows the
strength of all" (252). Sometimes three antitheses
can be found in one couplet (37-38, 54-55, 57-58).

Sometimes large paragraph units are developed in a series of images in antitheses (1-18, 54-62, 67-80, 101-10, 203-16). Sometimes the antithesis at the beginning and end helps unify a paragraph: "mount" and "drop" (19, 30).

In this epistle, Pope describes the dynamic complexity of man's psychology. He does so by showing how it is governed by two kinds of conflict — that between reason and passion within the individual, and that between the ruling passions of the individuals constituting society. Both oppositions are, however, in accordance with his dialectical view of nature, harmoniously synthesized so that a clear sense of order, despite the confusing complexity, eventually emerges for both the individual and the society of which he is a part.

Pope's first important point, as expressed in the contrasting details of a watch figure, is that self-love is the "spring" that provides the energy and reason is the "balance" that controls the beat (53-62). In other contrasting figures, Pope also states, but in mixed metaphors, that passion is a lawless meteor, an extremely active moving force; concerned with immediate pleasure, it devours greedily. But reason is, in contrast, a fixed plant; a passive check, concerned for the future and consequence, it tastes carefully (63-74, 89-90). Both reason and passion are absolutely necessary to human life; reason is the pilot, but passion is the driving wind (105-8). And both possess divine attributes — God is present in "storm" (passion) and "calm" (reason), Pope contends (109-10).

As for the passions themselves, Pope provides two types of synthesis and equilibrium for them. The first synthesis is made with reason. That is, the passions in conflict within the individual are harmonized or "well-accorded" by means of reason that, following Nature and God, imparts to passions a noble purpose. Thus, in Pope's words, as they are "mix'd and soften'd," they "in His [God's] work unite," and thereby "Make and maintain the balance of the mind" (111-20). Pope suggests a picture of dynamic psychological stability:

> *The lights and shades, whose well-accorded*
> *strife*
> *Gives all the strength and colour of our life.*
> (121-22)

The second method of synthesizing the passions involves somewhat more complicated processes. The different passions, depending upon the degree of pleasure experienced by the senses, are first synthesized into one master or ruling passion within one person (87-88, 123-32), a result to which reason even contributes through rationalization (149-58). Reason again, however, although it cannot entirely suppress, may certainly "rectify" (163) the ruling passion. That is, reason *and* the master passion, conjoined, produce good. It is in this manner that the fundamental principle of the *Essay*, "Th'Eternal Art educing good from ill" (175), operates. Reason, assisted by Nature operating according to this law, can transform the ruling passions into sources of powerful virtue. Anger, for example, is converted into zeal and fortitude, avarice into prudence, lust into love (the "strainers" represent the agency of reason), envy into emulation (185-92): "Nature gives us . . . the virtue nearest to our vice ally'd; Reason the byass turns to good from ill" (195-97). The total result of this synthesizing and transforming process is a state of equilibrium in which light and darkness and vice and virtue, good and evil motives, are so joined (Pope employs a painting metaphor of colors to illustrate the synthesis — "light and shade," "mix," "blend, soften, unite") that it is difficult to distinguish between them. Pope's solution for this moral problem is divine insight, the conscience or "the God within the mind" (204, 205-16).[6]

At the conclusion of the discourse, Pope provides a third synthesis, one, however, in which the operations of reason are not included. Reverting again to the major proposition stating the need for the whole view in order that the proper measure of individual parts can be taken — "Heav'n's great view is One, and that the Whole" (238)—Pope develops a social and psychological variation of the theme of the eternal rightness of things. Providence so operates in accordance with the good of the whole, he declares again, that all the conflicts and differences in the passions of the many individuals comprising society are neutralized and work out for the best, "the joy, the peace, the glory of Mankind" (248).[7] Variety in passion is given to men so that they will depend on each other for support: "one Man's weakness grows the strength of all" (252).[8] In the enforced social synthesis that follows, all classes and kinds of people, some in direct conflict, should cooperate happily: the learned and the foolish, the rich and the poor, the master and the servant. In this balanced social scheme, every state of being brings its own comfort and every age its appropriate passion. And so, to conclude with Pope's antitheses, self-love is converted into a benevolent virtue by this eternal "force divine," and Man possesses the "one comfort" in knowing that though he's "a fool, yet God is wise" (291-94).

In the second epistle, then, Pope's method of developing his argument resembles that of the first. Here Pope argues that the individual must correctly blend reason and passion in order to produce mental balance, and that only God and Nature can reconcile the conflicting ruling passions of individuals in order to effect an ordered and coherent society in which everyone cheerfully accepts his

place. His final view of social equilibrium parallels,
it is evident, the cosmic harmony in the first epistle.
But in both epistles, the precondition for concord—
psychological, social, or cosmic—is a merger of opposing forces. Now Pope is prepared for the har-
monies of the third and fourth epistles, where he
shows how self-love, a vice, is transformed into
sympathy, a virtue, the foundation for a benevolent
morality.

[iii]

IN THE third epistle, Pope employs about sixty-five
antitheses in a little over 315 lines, the proportion
remaining as high as in the previous two parts. Nor
is there anything unusual about the kind of antitheses Pope uses in this part of the poem. Sometimes he develops whole sections or paragraphs by
means of antitheses (1-26, 49-70 [man-animal];
79-98, 147-68 [state of nature-civilized state], 181-
88, 269-82, 283-302). Sometimes he uses images as
the basis for contrast (85-90, 147-68, 181-88); sometimes he packs many antitheses into a few lines
(206 [2], 143-44 [3], 254-56 [6]); at least once he
juxtaposes two opposites in one line (208). Particularly neat are the series of antitheses that contrast the ants and bees in their habitation (sub-
terranean - aerial), government (republic - monar-
archy), and economy (communism-free enterprise,
181-88), and the images that contrast the peaceful
state of nature and the warlike condition of con-

temporary civilization (147-68).

The two most significant themes of this epistle are expressed in two interrelated antitheses: reason and instinct, self-love and social love. Reason "that may go wrong" and instinct "that must go right" (94) are carefully and elaborately contrasted, and a military image serves to a large extent as the basis for tying together their opposing properties (85-90). The former, reason, is slow, heavy, fallible, requires will power and time for operation, and is not divinely inspired; but the latter, instinct, is quick, sure, infallible, requires no will power, and is divinely inspired (79-98). These two are tied to another opposing pair, self-love and social love. Pope's argument is somewhat ambiguous at this point; but the main lines are clear, made more pronounced by the antitheses. The force of love, Pope tells us, originates in a natural instinct. So animals of the same species mate instinctively with each other (121). In man this instinctive love is joined with reason that strengthens, extends, or improves its ties and bonds (133). In the original state of nature, self-love and social love had operated so harmoniously as to unify the whole creation in peace. Reason then imitated instinct, human beings learning from the animals and insects how to live. But in the course of time, tyranny and superstition brought irrational fear and hate. Yet throughout this corrupting process, self-love was still the pro-

pelling force (269-70). Only after self-love is converted into social by means of reason, reason that
recognizes the need for self-protection—"Forc'd
into virtue . . . by Self-defence" (279)—can there
be harmony in human society and government.
Thus the two opposing forces in this vision are
reconciled:

> *Self-Love forsook the path it first pursu'd,*
> *And found the private in the public good.*
>   (281-82)

In the "gen'ral frame" which takes in the whole
of the creation, Pope repeats for emphasis at the
very end his ideal vision of unity: God and Nature
have made "consistent" these "two motions" of the
soul, have "bade Self-Love and Social be the same"
(315-18).

Just as we expect, then, it is toward the end of
the discourse that Pope images this reconciliation
of opposites. But this time he images the fusion in
a noble musical synthesis expressive of his ideal—a
harmony in government that approximates that of
the original state of nature (283-302). In order to
bring about this result, the "Poet," as "Patriot" (so
Pope expresses the neoclassical conception of the
writer's function as legislator), "Re-lum'd" Nature's "ancient light" and thereby "taught People"
and "Kings" the proper "use of Pow'r."

> *Taught nor to slack, nor strain its tender*
>   *strings,*
> *The less, or greater, set so justly true,*
> *That touching one must strike the other too;*
> *'Till jarring int'rests of themselves create*
> *Th'according music of a well-mix'd State.*
>   (290-94)

One notes that each line, each idea, is balanced
with an antithesis. The rhetoric, as is usual in
Pope's best writing, dramatizes an equilibrium that
reinforces the conceptual statement. Such is the
"World's great harmony," Pope declares trium-
phantly, the harmony produced by the balanced
government of a limited monarchy, "Order, Union,
full Consent" (295-96). And this harmony of the
three estates—"Servant, Lord, or King"—parallels,
Pope concludes, that of the cosmic and natural system—"Beast, Man, or Angel" (302)—which he had
explained in the first epistle. In both, then, in the
natural cosmos and the man-made state, he sees
each part cooperating to one end, the good of the
whole.

[iv]

THE RELATIVELY few image complexes in the fourth
epistle are amply compensated and balanced by a
very large number of antitheses. Over ninety in 370
lines appear to emphasize Pope's fundamental
thesis that "All Nature's diff'rence keeps all Na-

ture's peace" (56). As is usual in Pope's practice,
most of the antitheses are expressed in single pairs
of words or phrases balanced and opposed within
the line of verse. Some lines, however, contain two
pairs of antitheses (4, 6, 68, 70, 94, 114, 162, 334,
380, 392); and some couplets contain two pairs
(241-42, 315-16, 323-24, 339-40, 375-76), and some
even three (23-24, 71-72). A few paradoxes also
appear—"The Learn'd are blind," "poor with fortune and with learning blind" (19, 329). And, finally, many paragraph units are also organized around
a series of antitheses (1-18, 19-28, 67-72, 137-46,
309-26, 327-40, 373-98).

In his discussion, Pope grounds a fixed and stable
happiness, the subject of this epistle, on that principle of nature which "Acts not by partial, but by
gen'ral laws"; therefore such happiness, he believes,
subsists "not in the good of one, but all." Further,
according to his argument, it must be "attainable
by all," "equal" and "social" (29-40, "Argument").
Should people think that fortune, on the other
hand, makes some happy and others unhappy,
heaven's balance, which takes into consideration
the long view and the good of the whole, equalizes
this condition—for those who are so happy suffer
"Fear," and those who are not gain "Hope" (67-70).
Although when we do take the long view we still
cannot be sure who is good, Pope continues, yet
he who follows Nature (29) and "God's whole

scheme below" (on earth) and accepts the principles that "partial Ill is universal Good" and
"Whatever Is, is Right" will in the long run be most
blessed (93-96, 114, 145).

Moreover, Pope argues, material things and
tangible earthly rewards bring no lasting happiness.
Only a spiritual quality, virtue, which invariably
produces a clear conscience, can be considered the
true source of enduring happiness in all men living
on earth. "The only point where human bliss
stands still" (311)—such is virtue, the universal
constant of human happiness, which is the result
of behaving charitably, benevolently. To Pope this
virtue is the amalgamating agent of all opposing
forces. And to him the best and clearest way to
describe the integrating synthesis which benevolence and sympathy can effect is by means of a
series of antitheses all centering on virtue—its un-
qualified goodness unmixed with ill (312); the
blessing it offers receiver and giver (314); the joy
it produces, win or lose, gaining its end or not
(315-16); its undiminishing value, no matter how
much of it there is (317); the greater pleasure its
compassionate tears give than does the laughter of
unfeeling folly (319-20); its quality, though always
exercised or active, of never being tired or ex-
hausted (322); its decent propriety, neither glad
when anyone suffers nor sad when anyone gains
(323-24). Such is the high point of the fourth

epistle, a paragraph largely developed by means of balanced antitheses.

But Pope does not stop here. He employs a further series of climactic antitheses to demonstrate that such virtuous happiness is not exclusive but takes in everyone and is broadly comprehensive (327-40). Thus he emphasizes once more the major theme of the entire essay: the proper union of the individual parts in the whole. This "sole bliss Heav'n could on all bestow" (327), he states; it comes to those who feel and think (328). It comes not to the bad, really poor despite their affluence and really blind despite their learning, but to the virtuous, Pope declares, although "untaught" (329-30). And the good, through "pursuing" Nature and the great chain that "links th'immense design, heaven, and earth . . . mortal and divine; Sees" that the happiness of one affects the happiness of all, "touches some above and some below" (336); learns from this unified vision of the coherent "Whole, The first, last, purpose of the soul; And knows," in conclusion, that "Faith, Law, Morals began" and will "end in love of God and love of Man" (339-40). Only the good man who realizes "Hope of known bliss," who realizes the potential for virtue, benevolence or brotherly love on earth, Pope insists, can also develop a sure "Faith in bliss unknown," can also achieve immortality in heaven (346), man's greatest happiness. So Pope crowns the structure of his moral system as he connects man's greatest virtue, love of God, with his greatest happiness, immortality (350). Pope, one sees, deliberately balances one antithesis upon another and moves toward an irrevocable and lasting reconciliation and equilibrium in a final all-comprehending synthesis through the agency of spiritual virtue, benevolence or love, which in his opinion is the only source of happiness on earth or in heaven.

Pope even views his art in the *Essay on Man* largely in terms of contrast. In the concluding peroration addressed to Bolingbroke, Pope describes how Pegasus, his inspired Muse, "now stoops, or now ascends To man's low passions, or their glorious ends" (375-76)—he refers here to the conversion through mutual dependence of self-love to social love and sympathy, the psychological basis of an ordered and coherent society. And, further, he confesses how Bolingbroke, who understands the whole, the variety, of nature (377), has taught his pupil Pope "to fall with dignity" (while writing realistically about the "low passions"), "with temper rise," and "to steer From grave to gay, from lively to severe" (378-80); that is, Bolingbroke has shown Pope how to blend contrasting tones in his discourse. Further, again, urged by Bolingbroke, Pope declares that he "turn'd" his numbers "From [empty] sounds to [substantial] things," from shallow and frivolous "fancy" to the profound sin-

cerity and sympathy of the "heart," thereby ele-
vating the truth of "Nature's light" instead of the
untrue imitations of "Wit's [Fancy's] false mirror"
(391-93).

Finally, in the concluding paragraph of the
fourth epistle, Pope sums up the major themes in
a series of fundamental syntheses that illustrate the
chief truths clearly seen in "Nature's light" — that
man errs, for whatever is in God's coherent system,
is right; that reason and passion cooperate to produce mental balance; that self-love and social love
are, in effect, the same (393-96). Pope achieves a
sense of order and repose through a comprehensive
reconciliation of the opposing concepts developed
in the essay. Rhetoric and logic cannot reinforce
each other more effectively.

[v]

A CONCEPTUAL synthesis of the real and the ideal, it
might be noted, governs the major syntheses in the
total structure of the *Essay on Man*. The first rep-
resents ugly and painful reality; the second, man's
hope for perfect happiness and divine love. Pope's
contention is that a limited and erring vision con-
strues the antithesis of the real and ideal as irreconcilable conflict. But his hopeful message is that we
should accept the real, "whatever is," because it
"is" as "right" as it ought to be when seen in Nature's light and as a part of God's comprehensive
plan for the creation. Ultimately, therefore, the real

is only nominal, for it will be translated into the ideal. Again, although Pope states that "Virtuous and vicious ev'ry Man must be" (II, 231), he does not mean that this antithesis expressing man's self-conflict is absolutely irreconcilable and that morality is thereby paralyzed. On the contrary, the context for the unpleasant reality of this psychological antithesis inherent in man's condition makes clear that it has to be considered in terms of the dynamic and comprehensive scheme of things of which it is a contributing part. Thus, because "Heav'n's great view is One, and that the Whole" (II, 238), this psychological reality is reconciled with the ultimate ideal of social harmony, a harmony in which man can paradoxically possess "happy frailties" (II, 241) and in which "one Man's weakness grows the strength of all" (II, 252). Likewise, the figure of real man, motivated by self-love and mixed with vice and virtue, is assimilated into a concluding image of man idealized "in one close system of Benevolence" (IV, 358), a system in which real man is idealized as he becomes one with God (IV, 361-72). Pope does not minimize stubborn reality. Nor does he flinch from the painful problems it poses. But he always works toward their solution in terms of the opposing ultimate ideal of perfect order and coherence, the result of God's love. Certainly, as we have noted before, his dialectic results in a not unusual religious orthodoxy.

Aesthetic contrast may also be considered the principle of arrangement that underlies the balanced structure of the *Essay* as a whole. That is, the first epistle, in which Pope takes a cosmic view of perfect peace and happiness in the whole planned by God in His infinite wisdom and love, contrasts with the second, in which he takes a mundane view of one part of God's creation, man and his psychological conflicts. Concentrating on the individual, the second, in turn, contrasts with the third, which describes the individual in nature and society. The fourth completes this spiraling movement by showing man operating in human society to his best advantage in order that he may produce through the virtue of sympathy an enduring happiness for himself and all around him on earth; and, at the same time man in this manner prepares for immortal happiness as he joins a benevolent God in heaven. In a sense, then, when he shows how virtuous man, by means of an altruistic love that knows no bounds, can be elevated to God and be assimilated in Him, Pope blends the last into the first and concludes on a note of perfect harmony.

Pope's expression is never diffuse, always elegantly neat, compact and condensed. For these formal effects the balanced antithesis is largely responsible. But the antithesis is not simply a superficial rhetorical artifice in the *Essay on Man*. It is,

rather, an essential device by means of which Pope
deftly structures the thought of the whole work
and thereby generates an attractively lively excitement. In each of the parts, a final reconciliation of
antagonistic and contradictory forces helps estab-
lish a delicately balanced equilibrium symbolizing
the complex order and coherence of God and Nature. It is largely because Pope believes the many
are assimilated into the one, and really puts into
practice what he believes, that the thought of the
Essay appears to be eclectic. Pope himself was
aware of what he was doing; and as his admission
in "The Design" makes clear, such must have been
the function of the structural synthesis: "If I
could flatter myself that this Essay has any merit,
it is in steering betwixt the extremes of doctrines
seemingly opposite . . . and in forming a *temperate*
yet not *inconsistent,* and a *short* yet not *imperfect*
system of Ethics" (p. 7, lines 20-24).

NOTES: III

1. All the antitheses in the *Essay on Man* are listed
   according to line number. Paragraphs or fairly
   large rhetorical units organized around a series
   of contrasts are followed by parentheses that indicate the individual antitheses. The text is that
   of the Twickenham edition, ed Maynard Mack
   (New Haven, 1951), Vol. III, Part i.

I — 1-16 (2, 6, 7, 8-10, 11, 12, 15, 16), 17, 32, 39-40,
   42, 51-52, 60, 61-68 (61-63, 61-62, 64, 65, 67, 68),
   69, 74, 75-76, 79, 88, 89, 90, 96, 99-112 (savage In-

dian and civilized Christian), 114, 116, 120, 140,
146, 152, 163, 172, 173-75, 182, 184, 184-88, 191,
193-96, 196, 206, 209-22 (209-10, 211-12, 213-14,
215-16, 220, 221-22), 223-26, 230, 235-36, 238, 240-
41, 241-42, 249-50, 267, 268, 270, 275, 276, 277-78,
279, 288, 289-92 (289, 290, 291, 292). Total: 70.

II — 1-18 (1-2, 4, 7, 8, 9, 10, 11-12, 13, 14, 15, 16, 17),
19 and 30, 37, 38, 42, 43-44, 48, 49, 52, 54-62 (54,
55, 56, 57-58, 59-60, 61-62), 63 and 65, 67-80
(67-70, 71-72, 73-74, 76, 80), 82, 91-92, 94, 101-10
(104, 102 and 105, 108, 109-10), 124-25, 126, 130,
140, 141, 149-50, 155, 158, 164, 172, 173, 175, 180,
196, 197, 198, 199-200, 201, 202, 203-16 (203, 208,
210, 212, 213-14), 231, 233, 235, 236, 243, 250, 252,
263-64, 265-66, 294. Total: 73.

III — 1-26 (2, 5, 6, 8, 13-14, 15-16, 21, 23, 24, 25), 48,
49, 49-70 (Man and Animals), 74, 79-98 (79, 82-86,
86-90, 91-92, 93, 94, 96, 97-98), 99, 100, 102, 126,
143-44, 147-68 (Nature and Civilization), 181-88
(181-82, 184, 185-88), 193-94, 206, 208, 240, 251,
254-56 (6 antitheses!), 261, 262, 269-82 (269,
270-71, 274, 275, 276, 278, 282), 283-302 (284, 287,
288, 289, 290, 291, 292, 297-98, 300, 302), 306, 309,
312, 316, 317-18. Total: 66.

IV — 1-18 (1, 4, 5, 6, 9-10, 13, 14, 16, 17, 18), 19-28 (20
21, 22, 23-24, 26), 36, 38, 44, 45, 48, 58, 59, 60, 64,
67-72 (68-70, 71-72), 83, 85, 86, 87, 88, 89-90,
91-92, 93, 105-6, 114, 119-20, 137-46 (137-38,
139-40, 141-42, 144, 146), 149, 156, 161, 162, 173-
74, 175, 180, 196, 199, 200, 201, 223, 233, 241-42,
254, 255, 257-58, 271-72, 290, 294, 297, 306, 308,

309-26 (312, 314, 315-16, 317, 319-20, 322, 323-24),
327-40 (327, 328, 329, 330, 334, 335, 338, 339-40),
346, 361, 371-72, 373-98 (375-76, 378, 380, 388,
392, 393, 395, 396). Total: 92.

2. The antitheses in this series reinforce the idea
   that Pope wishes to communicate—that Man, of a
   mixed nature, is in an equivocal position in
   the scale of being. Here also, the sharp antitheses
   add bite to the satire. Rebecca P. Parkin detects
   humor in them; see her book, *The Poetic Workmanship of Alexander Pope* (Minneapolis, 1955),
   p. 60.

3. Can we blame Voltaire for showing fatigue and
   crying out with exasperation his objection to this
   radical treatment of antithesis? See G. R. Havens,
   "Voltaire's Marginal Comments on Pope's *Essay
   on Man*," *MLN*, XLIII (1928), 431-32.

4. For an explication of "vindicate," see Henry
   Wasser, *The Explicator*, VII (Nov., 1948), 12.
   Milton's "justify" in *Paradise Lost* signifies de-
   fending or maintaining by force; Pope's "vindicate," on the other hand, signifies upholding by
   evidence or argument, by explaining rationally.

5. Note the two antitheses in the adverbs and verbs.

6. The provision for a conscience is Pope's answer
   to the charge of fatalism. Pope himself said, in a
   letter to Ralph Allen (8 September 1736), that
   the third stanza of his *Universal Prayer* was important because it "reconciles Freedom and Ne-
   cessity; and is at least a comment on some
   Verses in my Essay on Man, which have been

mis-construed." The third stanza of the version
he presented to Allen differs somewhat from
that which is ordinarily reprinted: "Yet [the
Great First Cause] gav'st us in this dark Estate/
To know the Good from Ill;/And, binding Nature
fast in Fate,/Left'st conscience free, and Will."—
The Correspondence of Alexander Pope, ed.
George Sherburn (Oxford: 1956), IV, 31-32.

7. This beatific vision Pope also sums up in the conclusion of the *Essay* (IV, 375-76), where he describes how his poetic muse "now stoops, or now
ascends,/To Man's low passions, or their glorious
ends."

8. Also repeated in III, 111-12: "God fram'd a
Whole, the Whole to bless,/On mutual Wants
built mutual Happiness."

IV

IMAGERY

*What vary'd being
peoples ev'ry star. . . .*
AN ESSAY ON MAN, I, 27

P OPE PROVIDES a figurative unity to his *Essay on Man* by means of balanced antitheses and certain reiterated images (the circular frame, nature's chain of being and love, the conversation, navigation). Pope also uses a great variety of additional images to develop his ideas in the course of pursuing his argument in this work. The great number of images (see Appendix for totals and tallies) definitely supports the contention that, for a work with difficult subject matter ordinarily given to the abstract speculation of philosophy, the *Essay* is substantially concrete. Considering for the moment only these images, the imaginative density of the didactic *Essay on Man* is remarkable. The four discourses are crowded with them; were they to be removed, only the bare skeleton of argument should remain. Hence, if only because they are quantitatively so significant, the images of this poem are worth careful study. It is the general nature and function of these images constituting a great proportion of the total, not the relatively small number of reiterated and integrating images, which will be discussed here.[1]

In this discussion, the word *image* refers to the sensory content of the poetry, including the literally descriptive, such as concrete details in illustrations or analogies; the figurative, such as similes,

metaphors, and personification; or the nominally
meaningful, such as names of people or things—
what Pope sometimes called *examples* or *pictures*
if they referred to people. With regard to his use of
the word *pictures*, Pope may have been harking
back to the old Renaissance sense of image as *icon*,
meaning a picture of something.[2] Yet no matter
how used, in the broad modern sense or the limited
traditional sense of the iconic, the image connotes
the sensuous.[3] This quality endows literature with
passion and a certain vividness that permit it to
fight the destructiveness of time and to outlast
the changes of rhetorical fashion. So we have our
chief reason for paying attention to the way in
which Pope uses imagery in *An Essay on Man*.
For a good deal of whatever animation the poem
now possesses for readers is to be found in its
imagery. Nor did Pope himself think of it as a
veneer of the superficially ornamental, as a hasty
reading of his "Design" of the poem may lead some
to believe.[4] For without imagery, according to the
view that the essence of literature is distilled from
image and figure, his verse could not rise to the
level of poetry. This he well knew as a practicing
poet, although his intention was, as he modestly
says in a letter to Swift (1 December 1731), to
"make mankind less Admirers, and greater Reasoners."[5]

[i]

To demonstrate the importance of imagery in the *Essay on Man*, all we need do is to summarize the imaginative "action" of the poem. Let us look closely, then, at the first part. Generally, here, in the first epistle, Pope organizes his ideas by means of analogy, employing such figures as the simile or metaphor and developing them in large blocks or paragraphs. Thus, for example, at the beginning Pope addresses his friend Bolingbroke and imagines, in two metaphors, that their discussion of moral philosophy will take in a panoramic view of man in nature, a garden or wilderness, and be a hunt after quarry (I, 5-14). Through the imagery that Pope provides, we must imagine the two moralists out of doors enjoying the country scene; and, soon, when night falls after the hunt, they see the stars emerge. In the next few paragraphs, the splendor and overwhelming immensity of the scenic universe are suggested by an image of wheeling constellations of planets in a vast frame or machine pulled taut by the attraction of the links in a great chain (I, 19-32, 33-4, 45-8). This mechanical frame is beyond puny man's comprehension, Pope declares; being but a point in space, man cannot completely understand his role in the vast scheme of things. He is, indeed, like a wheel in a huge clockworks (I, 51-60), or like blind and dumb beasts, such as the horse and ox, made to serve masters

whose will they cannot completely comprehend
(I, 61-8).

Man is partially blind, Pope continues, able to
read only one page of the Book of Fate, and depend-
ent for greater perceptiveness upon God and the
great teacher Death (I, 77-94). Man is as blind as a
lamb being fed before slaughter (I, 81-4), and has
only the hope of immortality in heaven, like the
simple savage Indian (I, 99-112). Man is not a
judge—he cannot complain of God's injustice and
put himself in the scales against God, for obviously
the scales of justice will not balance man's opinion
against God's providence (I, 113-22). Nor is man to
think that he is like a powerful, proud, and imperi-
ous king, the center of beneficent nature (I, 131-40);
for nature is also destructive and man is forced to
suffer (I, 141-63). At this point of his argument
for general Providence and *against* particular Provi-
dences, Pope supplies a series of images to illustrate the beneficent and destructive powers of impartial nature.

Pope then pictures man in a middle state between the angel and the fly or mite, with senses
proportioned to the level of his being (I, 173-206).
Here, again, he provides a series of figures to illustrate the several senses and their appropriate limitations, a series of images that provides a transition
to the next block, a further series of sensuous images
that illustrate the scale or ladder of the senses in

accordance with nature's chain of being (I, 207-30, 232-46). Should this ladder of being break, Pope imagines a disorder that resembles the apocalypse but which he pictures in familiar astronomical terms (I, 251-6). Lastly, man, Pope says, must not impiously rebel against the dread eternal order, just as the parts of the body must not aspire to higher functions. For God is like the mind that controls all the subordinate parts of the body; each has its own job to do (I, 259-76).

The whole argument in the first epistle, it is clear, is developed by means of large image blocks—about thirteen altogether. Pope works carefully, deliberately, and neatly from idea to image, strengthening his thought with examples and illustrations: a large frame or machine that contains a plurality of worlds, the frame being supported by the chain of being made up of an infinity of links held together by gravitation or attraction; an enormous clockworks of wheels within wheels; a book of countless pages; God, the judge of all, holding the scales of justice; a scale or ladder of being and senses, with man on the middle rung; the several parts of the body controlled by the mind; and other less important supporting images.

Pope cannot be coolly abstract; he must use concrete details to provide visual excitement. When he thinks of the idea of justice, especially man's complaint against the injustice of God, he presents a full image of the scales of justice ("scale," "weigh," "balance," "rod"; I, 113-21), shows the scale in operation, and projects his feelings through the image. This method, that of an imaginative writer, is dynamic and dramatic. Perhaps, however, his method with such a traditional symbol as scales of justice is not quite so effective among contemporary readers biased by the demands of a fashion that favors a different type of metaphor, but it is certainly effective in those passages where through close observation of natural details he can provide sharp and original sensuous images that transcend fashions in rhetoric. For example, the scientific details of the rose and its "effluvia" or exhalations (I, 199-200) and of the spider's touch (I, 217-8) are exquisitely treated, both vividly animated with picture and sound, and both retaining their freshness to this day.[6]

Furthermore, since his major theme is the fullness of nature, Pope offers a great range in the diversity of particular images in his first epistle to illuminate this generalization. For astronomical effects, all noted for their sublimity and grandeur, he refers to the Newtonian immensities of the ethereal frame (I, 270) and its wheeling constellations, whole systems in the universe, the "argent fields" and "solar walks" of the milky way and the stars, the sun and planets and their satellites. On earth he sees a variety of animals and vegetation to illustrate the plenitude of the great chain of being. Among the four-footed beasts are such domestic brutes as the horse, ox, lamb, dog, bull, pig; and such wild animals as the bear, lion, mole, lynx, elephant. Pope also cites birds, such as the sparrow; reptiles, especially the lowly worm; and fish in general. Among the insects that appear are the fly (perhaps the butterfly), mite, spider, and bee. As for vegetation, he notes weeds and flowers, but points only to one species, the rose; of fruit, he mentions the grape; and he also mentions poisonous herbs and trees such as the oak. He includes such natural details as atoms and bubbles; earth, sea, ocean, and rill; air and wind; earthquakes, tempests, and dew.[7] Even microscopic objects are not overlooked. At the other extreme of the chain are the angels. Pope refers often to them and to spirits in the first epistle, for they are necessary links in his argument; but he does not stop to visualize them closely, except to remark that they have wings and burn with rapture. On the other hand, man is pictured with his senses—sight, touch, smell, and hearing—and with his head, hair, hand and heart. All these natural details amply demonstrate the plenitude of the creation. When they are catalogued, we are surprised to note the heterogeneity of the numerous images of nature that Pope has packed into his neatly compressed verses.

In the following epistles, Pope's method of developing his argument by means of vivid imagery remains the same. In almost every paragraph Pope focuses upon an image, analogy or illustration, simile or metaphor, thereby demonstrating once more the fundamental importance of imagery. Thus, to validate this point, we can quickly review the elaborate "pictures" Pope projects in the second epistle: a topographical metaphor of puzzled man trapped on an isthmus (3-18); the proud Newtonian astronomer studying in the great frame the movements of the spheres but foolish before the elemental and unfathomable mysteries of the mind (19-42); science, personified, wearing the fashionable dress of vanity and pride (42-52); the traditional dualism, reason and passion, operating harmoniously in the figure of a mechanical watch with spring and balance (59-62); the mistaken efforts of chop-logic scholastics to separate reason and passion rather than to unite them (81-6); a weather metaphor of God and Nature responsible equally for reason and passion (102-10); the need to blend passions as a painter mixes colors[8] (111-12); a ruling passion that, like an uncontrollable malignancy, undermines health (135-46); ruling passion—as powerful as a court favorite of a weak queen, or an armed rebel before a weak judge, or a distemper gathered into a gout (149-60); the variety of ruling passions like varying winds determining destination (165-74); a mixed metaphor of

alchemy and horticulture (grafting) to show how
ruling passions mix and blend to produce good
(175-94); thus the difficulty of distinguishing good
from evil passions as in a painting with fine shad-
ing[9] (203-16); again the difficulty of fixing the
bounds of moral norms, especially vice, illustrated
with geographical allusions (221-30). Finally, Pope
concludes with a few more images: the variety of
ruling passions in all orders and ranks of men and
in all kinds of individuals imaged as contributing to
Heaven's great view, the whole, and thereby working out for the best (231-70); man supplied with
appropriate passions as he is seen progressing
through the five acts of a drama (271-82); man
deluded by pride and opinion as a painting may de-
ceive by appearances (283-6); and, as a last satiric
thrust, man behaving like a happy drunken fool
before the wisdom of God (288-94).

The large image complexes in the second discourse, many and varied, are not made to cluster
around any single metaphor, such as the important
chain of being and the frame of nature in the first
epistle. Yet again, although this may be true, it
must be admitted that Pope develops in the second epistle every important idea of his theme by
means of graphic imagery:

> *Th'Eternal Art educing good from ill,*
> *Grafts on this Passion our best principle.*
> (II, 175-76)

He uses a variety of common details taken from
ordinary life: disease and medicine, painting, grafting trees,[10] alchemy, drink, watch machinery,
navigation in a storm, dress. Pope draws these
images from such a variety of sources that when the
abstractions concerning man's mind are seen
against a rich background of reality, they are given
an added dimension of depth and an air of vivid immediacy. But although the images are realistic and
familiar, topical allusions are missing. Of course,
this general (but not complete) neglect of the contemporary, in so far as it indirectly enhances the
lasting significance of its statement, may be quite
proper to the supposed lofty dignity of a philosophic poem.

True, as it has been rightfully objected, the second epistle "is not remarkable for its poetical beau-
ties. Its language is mostly that of argument and
simple illustration." Another way of voicing this
objection is to say that Pope uses figures "in such
a way that they do not disturb a logical surface of
statement."[11] This effect is probably the result of
contrast with the first epistle. For there is in the
second nothing like the sustained grandeur of the
ethereal imagery of the first. But it is the very simplicity and homeliness of much of this imagery that
commends it to us. Sometimes, moreover, the visual
effects take us by surprise with their grandeur and
force — navigation in a storm (II, 104-10), society

and the five ages of man (II, 239-82), and the vivacious personification "In Folly's cup still laughs the bubble joy" (II, 288). Pope also achieves a solid compactness of vision in the concluding lines that only he is capable of:

> *See the blind beggar dance, the cripple sing,*
> *The sot a hero, lunatic a king;*
> *The starving chemist in his golden views*
> *Supremely blest, the poet in his muse.*
>   (II, 267-70)

The last line contains a graphic and delicious ambiguity that makes us wonder if Pope is employing irony on himself.

In the third epistle, Pope uses large image complexes to develop the same theme as the first, that of the Part and the Whole, but here his emphasis is on Man acting his Part for the good of society as a Whole. He begins his discussion by noting that such is the case in nature where, in the chain of love, every part, as in gravitation or magnetism, is attracted to its neighbor (7-26), and every living thing, animal or vegetable, has its proper place and serves, not man, but its proper function in the unified whole: birds such as the lark, linnet, and goose; other animals such as the horse, steer, hog, bear; and plants. But of all animals, *e.g.*, insect-eating jay and predatory hawk, only man is capable of compassion and charity (49-70). Animals are governed by instinct, man by reason; yet instinct, being close to nature, is surer, like the volunteer sharpshooter (84-94). As before, Pope provides many images of nature to illustrate the sure operations of instinct among birds, spiders, and storks (99-108).[12] All animals, including man, are bound together by love, as individuals and as species (109-46). Such love underlay the original condition of man in nature; and at this point Pope presents a vivid image of innocent worship in the state of nature, the reign of God (147-60). His image of natural religion pictures a Golden Age with primitivistic overtones: original natural society as pastoral and vegetarian. But in the post-lapsarian state, man became a butcher of animals and turned against his own species (161-68). In a series of images taken from nature, Pope, the romantic naturalist, then demonstrates how man's reason is instructed by the instinct of the creatures of nature — birds and beasts, and such insects as the ant, bee, and spider; and even the lowly Nautilus helps! (169-98) [12] And so political societies originated among men. True religion has its origin in the natural principle of love; but superstition, after "Wit oblique" had broken that steady natural light (a prism image: 232), operated on fear and produced horrible tyrannies, religious persecution, and war (251-68). At this point the images of fanaticism are very vivid, ob-

viously demonstrating Pope's distaste for zeal in
religion and preference for the moderation of natural religion and ethical deism. But the poet as patriot, Pope declares, brought man back to the moral
principles of nature and God, and, in an archetypal
image, "relit her ancient light" (287). In a musical
image Pope pictures the reconciliation of social
opposites, "jarring interests," that constitute
"th'according music of a well-mixed State," like
"the World's great harmony" (289-96). All social
and natural forces are balanced on one point (301).
So, to conclude in two similes, the love of the vines
and the elm and the two motions of the planets,
Pope argues his thesis that man is activated by a
synthesis of opposing kinds of love, self and social
(311-16).[13]

So, again, Pope works out his moral argument
through detailed images. As noted before, he never
stops at abstraction; he always cites concrete in-
stances and offers vivid illustrations. We can agree
with John Aikin who observed that the third
epistle "is highly poetical. Dwelling more upon illustration than reasoning, it has drawn from a variety
of sources pictures of beauty and sublimity, coloured
with all the splendour of language proper to the
author."[14] In this epistle, the most numerous images
are drawn from external nature; it is especially rich
in animal imagery, perhaps even richer than the
first: wild and domesticated beasts — horse, fawn,

steer, hog, bear, mole; birds — lark, linnet, jay, hawk, falcon, dove, stork, eagle, goose, and the migratory flight and nesting habits of birds; insects — the spider and its web, ants and their hills, bees and their hives; fish or animals of the sea — the little nautilus; reptiles — worm. The second epistle has only a few animal images; the fourth has one.

The fourth epistle is unlike the other parts of the poem in that its imagery is not so richly detailed. Pope does not use very many image complexes to structure his paragraphs. For the most part, he refers to names, alluding to historical figures, past and present. However, the epistle opens with an apostrophe to happiness figured in an elaborate agricultural metaphor (7-16).[15] Other significantly elaborate images that contribute to vivid structural effects and that, therefore, deserves mention are a business metaphor (85-92), a clothing metaphor (193-204) — a particularly lively and colorful section; a counting house metaphor that begins and ends a long paragraph (269-72, 305-8). Closing the argument is a naturalistic image of ever widening circles of altruism that begin in self-love, a pebble dropped in still water, and end in a comprehensive love like God's, a vast circle that embraces the whole of the natural creation. So Pope simply and movingly ends his argument as he sees the possibility of paradise on earth (361-72). In the closing peroration of the essay, Pope mixes two images. He pictures his muse in flight (375-78) and Bolingbroke as a pilot leading him and his little boat to fame in posterity (379-90). For Bolingbroke taught his disciple to turn from the fanciful imitations of art, "Wit's false mirror," to the truths of nature, "Nature's light" (391-93).

There are certain obvious differences between the imagery of the fourth epistle and that of the others. Because this discourse is more intensely devoted to an ethical problem — man's search for happiness, Pope refers but once to animals, a dog. As in the third epistle, which is devoted to a social problem, the images of nature in the fourth are rare: seeds, seaweed, and apples. Nature is only seen archetypically as a road or path, or as light and sunshine. Relative to the other epistles, the fourth, therefore, clearly lacks natural sensuousness. But what it lacks in one area it makes up in another; allusions to human beings, general or particular, abound. So Pope refers in general to learned philosophers, kings and queens, tyrants and their favorites and subjects, madmen and fools, a syphilitic father and his worried son, cobbler, saint, friar, monk, parson, bandit, whore, hermit, judges and senators, and an Indian. In particular he refers to such historical figures as Alexander the Great, Caesar, Titus, Cicero, Socrates, Aurelius, Marcellus, Charles XII, Prince Eugene, Calvin, Bacon, Crom-

well, Falkland, Turenne, Sidney, Bishop of Mar-
seilles, Lucrece, Abel and Cain, and such contemporaries as his mother, his friends, Bethel, Digby,
Bolingbroke, and that notorious rapist, Francis
Chartres.

Only a few large extended or focal metaphors in
this fourth discourse possess visual interest: the
seed of happiness (7-16), clothing and occupations
(193-204), the pebble of self-love and the waves of
love (361-72), the pilot of the little bark along the
stream of time (379-86). As a result, the impression
is that this part is the least imaginative, the most
prosaic, of the four.

[ii]

What can be said of the imagery in *An Essay on
Man* as a whole, of Pope's methods of developing
his themes by means of concrete details and figures,
the simile, metaphor, and allusion?

First, the range and variety of images are strik-
ing. Except for three images — the major conversation and circular frame of nature, which symbolizes
God's infinitely loving embrace, the minor navigation, and the important structural antithesis —
Pope does not maintain a single figurative view
throughout the whole essay or within any one
epistle. Generally, the vast majority of images are
used to structure the paragraph,[16] or they are used
for brief illustrations in a couplet or two. Unrolling
the vast panorama of nature and society, Pope

operates like a modern motion-picture photographer who focuses sharply and rapidly on one series of images after another, his order controlled not so much by the logic of metaphor as it is by the logic of argument. The images, considered by themselves without reference to the ordering thread of prose argument, appear to be discrete, the effect diffuse and scattered. Pope's writing may thus lack intensity; yet it is also true that rapidly shifting images animate the style, enhancing a quality of the images themselves. For such is Pope's manner, the light rococo, witty, lively, and sparkling.

Since his major theme is Nature, only through numerous vivid images of natural objects of phenomena could Pope hope to impress his readers with the reality of his moral vision, that man is only one species of being among many in the material universe. Thus Pope instills awe and admiration for the mysterious energy of Nature by visualizing it, as he had formerly done in the *Essay on Criticism*, as a divine archetypal *light* that provides the proper direction on a *walk, way, path,* or *road;* or by personifying it as the archetypal fecund mother with her many children and as the archetypal wise teacher; or by simply denominating it *great;* and finally, by dignifying it as he ascribes to it a force like God's and a body with God as its soul and describes it as the source of religious faith and morality, of man's hope in immortality, of patriarchal

government and monarchy, but not, Pope is spe-
cific, of the divine right of kings. Nature is also personified with a variety of other attractive and en-
dearing traits: it is simple, kind, genial (genera-
tive), plastic, quick, and vigorous; wild yet abiding
by law and order, fixed, stable, and unchanging.
The clearly-defined order and the enormous fe-
cundity, vitality, and variety of Nature are figured
in the splendid metaphor of the great chain of being. Thereby Pope can image the plenitude of dynamic Nature taking an infinity of forms, ranging
from one extreme of the scale to the other—among
animals, from the elephant to the insect mite, from
the high-flying eagle to the crawling worm; among
vegetation, from the majestic oak tree to the lowly
weeds and seaweed; among material things from
vast systems or constellations to bubbles and tiny
atoms; among the phenomena of natural events,
from mighty tempests and lightning and earthquakes to the quiet calm; among men, the imperial
race, from the proud and powerful to the humble
and weak, the rich to the poor, the king to the
cobbler.[17]

Of course, the *Essay on Man* does not pretend to
be a scientific treatise on astronomy and natural
history. It is, however, primarily a collection of
essays drawing upon the findings of science to validate certain moral propositions about Nature and
Man. Thus, although a reader of the eighteenth

century conditioned to accept the myth of the great chain may feel convinced that the scope of images is wide enough to validate Pope's moral vision, there are yet omissions within the chain that some scientific readers today undoubtedly cannot overlook. Certainly, the system of gradation leaves much to be desired. Such is the dissatisfying vagueness of the image of angels, spirits, and beings ethereal. The supernatural world is never documented with such concrete details as the natural world of animals, plants, and man. Really, as the distribution of the imagery proves, the great chain beyond man's link almost immediately fades away into the mystery of space. But even Locke experienced difficulty with angels. To say the least, therefore, the study of beasts is far more intensive than that of angels.[18]

Another omission is social in scope. Pope, in considering man, does not confront us with different races, types of civilization, or nationalities. The only exceptions are two brief references to the religion of the humble and simple savage, the American Indian, who is used for satiric contrast with the improperly civilized, proud, greedy and cruel Christian Europeans. Pope also neglects sexual differences, but this deficiency he supplied in a later moral essay on women. It is also easy to see that Pope gives a much more satisfying and full picture of the animal creation than he does of the plant kingdom.

Compared with animals, plants are infrequently
mentioned, rarely specified. The rose, oak tree,
seeds, vine, grape, grain, weeds and seaweed —
that is about all Pope does cite, unless we wish to
add two grafting images. Moreover, although he
does mention storms and tempests, Pope does not
linger over their description. Again, he mentions
a "wilderness," but he does not present a full scenic
description of wild areas of nature. Winter pros-
pects are not touched on. Clearly, Pope's picture of
nature is somewhat unbalanced.

Second, Pope's images in the *Essay on Man* are
general far more often than individualized. If occasionally concrete particulars or details are used,
they are expository — they strengthen the larger
sense of the universal truth, by exemplifying the
moral or by illustrating the generalizations concerning nature.[19]

So Pope deals often with the species mankind
(in which he includes womankind at least once: II,
190), and such diverse general types that take in
the sage and wit, fool, knave, rich and poor, hero,
proud and humble, youth and age, cripple, sot, lu-
natic, and ideal honest man (IV, 248); and such
occupational groups that include the politician and
courtier, preacher, poet, scientist, academic logician,
learned philosopher, doctor, starving chemist, and
merchant.

But when Pope occasionally singles out a partic-

ular individual, a Borgia or a Catiline, Caesar or
Alexander the Great, this person is meant to be
typical of evil men who, despite themselves, perform
God's will in the total scheme of things. When he
points to a Newton, the mathematician is supposed
to be typical of proud scientists whose knowledge
has obvious limits; or to a Nero, typical of passionate men who could have become good like a Titus;
or to a Demoivre, typical of mathematical genius
which is equaled by the spider's natural instinct
(III, 104); or to a Digby, typical of men who died
young, or to a Turenne, typical of men who died
old, both not because of excess of virtue but because
of chance; or to a blameless Bethel, typical of virtuous men suffering in a climate controlled by the
unvarying laws of nature.[20] Perhaps the only exception is Viscount Bolingbroke, who is individualized and presented as himself, the guide, philosopher, and friend of the poet (IV, 390). But even he,
too, is once used to point a political moral — the
vanity of superior talents (IV, 259-68). At the
Essay's beginning, Bolingbroke is not yet resigned
to the contemplative life and still appears to be
ambitious of worldly success (I, 1-2); however, at
the end, he appears to be happy, contented with
retirement from politics and the court (IV, 18).

Further, when Pope mentions a particular place,
York, the River Tweed, the Orkney Islands, Scot-
land, Zembla, or Greenland, it is for the purpose of

illustrating a moral generalization — the difficulty
of finding the extremes of vice (II, 221-24). Or when
he particularizes on the senses of living things, insects, beasts, and men, it is for the purpose of illustrating their appropriate limitations or their extremes in sensitivity as parts of the orderly chain
of being.[21]

Pope, to adapt a phrase from Blake, does meet
the mountains more than once — four times as a
matter of fact — but nothing great is done about it.
In general, the mountains in the *Essay on Man*
symbolize piles of money and a moral truth, or
they erupt or topple during earthquakes to illustrate the operations of General Providence, that
is, of nature according to law. It is as if Pope never
in his life really saw a very high and rugged moun-
tain that he could esthetically admire or enjoy—and
this *may be* a fact.[22] It *is* a fact that in this *Essay*
he takes no pleasure in their contemplation.

Although his theme is Nature in the *Essay*, Pope
does not linger over natural description. His sense
impressions, varied, numerous, and adapted to his
neat couplets, are characterized by swiftness, economy, and clarity of outline. Only too often as with
his *Pastorals*, Pope stops at naming objects and
abstracting from their chief qualities or characteristics appropriate epithets that bring certain essential details sharply to the attention. Yet again, the
generalizing and leveling effect of this method is

the same: the species, or the group or type, appears to be emphasized. Thus, for the beasts of the animal world, Pope employs such combinations as "dull ox," "proud" or "bounding steed," "groveling swine," "faithful dog," "half-reasoning elephant"; for birds: "ascending lark," "aerial eagle," "pampered goose," "stooping falcon"; for reptiles: "vile worm"; for insects: "spider's touch," "nice bee," "green myriads in the peopled grass."

This method of generalizing by means of epithets carries over into his description of the details of natural scenery: "latent tracts," "giddy heights," "mighty maze," "purling rill," "vernal wood," "painted" or "gilded clouds," "flowery lawn," "balmy" or "healing dew," "poisonous herbs," "gen-'rous vine," "waving tree"; and into descriptions of mankind, "man's imperial race": "merchant's toil," "sage's indolence," "monk's humility," "hero's pride," "proud man," "bandit fierce," "caverned hermit"; and into his personifications: "old Ocean," "Folly's cup," "unfeeling Folly," "whispering Zephyr," "Virtue's prize," "Virtue's tears," "Wit's false mirror," "Nature's light," and such metaphors as Nature's "path," "road," "way," or "walk."

Occasionally, but not often enough, this method produces a bold metaphorical periphrasis, such as the concentrated "iron harvests" and the two Miltonic images, "argent fields above" and "juice nectareous" (honey and wine). Another that has a

certain metaphorical brilliance is "pompous shade."
But in general the use of epithets produces an
apparent sharpness of definition and a measure of
control that permit Pope to describe natural phenomena with economy and dispatch and to place
the animals and insects easily in the chain. Still
from the modern point of view, this practice may
be too neat, too pat, as it expresses the essence of
an object, and the danger is that the facile formula
may stereotype and inhibit original and close observation.

The use of epithets, however, has classical precedent.[23] Operating upon the fundamental principle
of art as imitation, Pope, the neoclassical tradition-
alist, must believe that recognition is more valuable
than romantic novelty. A didactic intention may
also encourage the use of these generalizing epithets. Yet the result is the same, whether abstracting the essential epithet or emphasizing the moral;
for a kind of leveling follows upon the generalizing.
It is as if the poet were deliberately avoiding a
splash of subjective feeling and depersonalizing the
images which may express his response to nature.
So Pope, it is felt, definitely does not identify with
nature, brood over it, melt into it, or seek commu-
nion with it.[24] Probably related to this depersonal-
ization is a curious absence of color words in the
Essay. Pope's background, or "Nature's light,"
appears to be a sharply contrasting black-and-white.

or a neutral non-color like grey, shades that are in harmony with the bleak picture of cosmic optimism that he presents. Only very rarely does he use other colors — such as green for nature. (I, 210-213, 215), or gold and yellow for money (IV, 279, 296), or silver for moonlit sky (I, 41: "argent skies"). Indeed, as already mentioned, clarity of outline is made possible with such backgrounds; but what is sacrificed for distinctness is warm and rich sensuousness. Even when he uses painting metaphors — and there are three (II, 117-22, 208-14, 283-86) — Pope refers to light-shade and white-black in two; and in the third gold is used, but as part of an image of foolish deception. In the *Essay on Man,* Pope demonstrates no keen delight in color.[25]

In sum, the images of external nature in the *Essay on Man* are not decorative, not (in Pope's words) "One glaring Chaos and wild heap of Wit" (*EC,* 292). But they are utilitarian and narrowly functional: they enforce the moral; they serve to explain the logic of argument, and to validate, illuminate, and quicken the general truths of nature. This feature of his style, often described by critics, Pope himself noted in his remarks to Dr. Arbuthnot: after his work on the *Essay on Man,* he says, he "stoop'd to Truth and moraliz'd his song."[26] But it should also be recognized that although Pope invariably places his natural particulars within a moral frame, he did not completely desert "Fancy's

Maze." He may have deserted *pure description*, but not that type of description which has a moral reference, or, as he himself said "Sense" *(Ep. to Arb.,* 340-41, 148). Thus the only correct conclusion is that Pope does respond to nature, does present images of nature, but also that he decorously fuses them with a didactic purpose. As a matter of fact, the illustrative figures, similes and metaphors and concrete particulars, give Pope's expression whatever air of vivid immediacy they possess — "Life, Force, and Beauty"; and as they animate it and bring it at the same time close to ideal Nature, "the Source, and End, and Test of Art" *(EC,* 72-73), they become real and necessary adjuncts of his naturalistic theme. Without them this theme should have little or no emotional impact. As Bonamy Dobrée has recently written, its sensuous appeal and imaginative evocation help Pope's discourse achieve validity: "wherever Pope succeeds in teaching, it is by purely poetic means, by sharpening our apprehension."[27]

Third, Pope's images in the *Essay on Man,* as in the *Essay on Criticism,* are common and familiar, drawn, as a rule, not from esoteric learning but from everyday life. Hence, whatever esthetic pleasure they give, as in the case of his epithets, is owing to recognition. Not being original, they do not surprise or shock. Not being difficult or obscure, they persuade easily, contribute to the clarity of the

argument, and reinforce the moral realism of the
theme.[28] Thus, when he wishes to describe the pin-
nacle of spiritual happiness — "Virtue's prize," he
sees it as "The soul's calm sunshine" which cannot
be corrupted by external properties; and then he
seasons this bland archetypal image with his usual
dash of caustic satire, familiar images taken from
life:

> ... *A better would you fix?*
> *Then give Humility a coach and six,*
> *Justice a Conq'ror's sword, or Truth a gown,*
> *Or Public Spirit its great cure, a Crown.*
>   (IV, 168-72)

Such images are public; they are not dredged up
from the deep wells of the unconscious. On the
contrary, they lie lightly on the surface of con-
sciousness. Their very realism and availability presuppose a no-nonsense type of reader who is firmly
attached to this world and who tolerates not the
wild, daring, or fantastic, but only solid good sense.
The danger is that such common images may make
the expression vulgar and insipid, may render too
easy a difficult metaphysics. This is a very real
problem for Pope's style in the philosophic *Essay
on Man;* and as a result this work has been criti-
cized for indecorum in several places, for failing to
maintain the proper tone of awe and wonder that
should accompany a serious subject.[29] But in de-

fence of Pope's practice, it may be said that these
images are appropriate to the conversational tone
that Pope cultivates (along with the dramatic
framing image of conversation that integrates the
whole poem). Thus Pope was apparently unwilling
to sustain the sublime for long. It is, however, correct to say that these realistic images taken from
everyday life contrast with the sublimity of the
astronomical images of nature, and those are concentrated in the first epistle.

Pope's images of external nature, many of which
have already been mentioned, are also not remote
or exotic. Taken from scenes of cultivation close-by,
and within reach of the daily experience of his readers, they are supplemented by images from daily
life: watchspring and balance, compass, scale, book,
pulley, wheels, rattle and bauble; ladder, chain, and
links; path, road, walk, way; prism, carriage or
coach and six, gibbet, ribbands (honors), a pebble
dropped in still water, the last having an artless and
commonplace simplicity that is profoundly persua-
sive in the context, the very conclusion of the argument in the fourth epistle.

Further, to illustrate this generalization about
the familiar images in the *Essay on Man*, Pope
draws pictures from hunting and horsemanship,
gardening and horticulture (such as grafting),
painting, the court (but nothing elaborate), navigation and the weather (tempests, lightning, earth-

quakes), and games (bowling and hurling). He images the human body and refers to diseases (gout, cancer) and their treatment. He is concerned with clothing, money, and property, especially in the fourth epistle on earthly happiness. As already noted, sublime cosmic and scientific images are located in the first discourse, and they are inspired by visions of astronomy and Newtonian gravitation; thereafter, but with a few significant exceptions such as "aether" (III, 115-18), "empyreal sphere" (II, 23-4), "ethereal vault" (III, 263), among a few others,[30] Pope limits himself to those commonplaces of science derived from alchemy and the humors.

Pope's few allusions to the Bible do not conflict with this familiar tone; and, besides, these images constitute only a tiny proportion of the total number. There are no allusions to Jesus Christ or to Messianic doctrines fundamental to revealed religion or Christianity — Old and New Testament miracles, the Resurrection, the Trinity, and the Incarnation. Nor is Pope's conception of the origin of sin taken from the Scriptures in Genesis, the source of the concept of Adam's original sin and fall from grace. For Biblical myth Pope has substituted the myth of the great chain, the result being in the *Essay on Man* a secularization of imagery.[31] Therefore it is correct to say that the imagery in this poem is secular, suitable for a broad system of common sense ethics for laymen. And the numerous references to God, all part of his moral argument, are not associated with a tone of ecstatic and mystical devotion, except perhaps for the very last instance in the image of man's love rising to the level of God's (the circles of altruism). Pope clearly lacks the brooding devotional tone; he appears to be too unhesitantly cocksure as he aggressively asserts his argument. But this is not to deny that Pope stresses the mystery of human life in God's overall plan, one of those ultimate mysteries which, because of the limitation of reason, man must take on faith.

Probably the only intellectual difficulty raised by the imagery in the *Essay on Man* could have been the many allusions to classical figures, philosophers and politicians: Nero, Titus, Catiline, Decius, Curtius, Plato, Plotinus, Sceptics and Stoics in the second part; Epicurus, Democritus, Protagoras, Empedocles, Caesar, Titus (again), Aurelius, Marcellus, Socrates, Cicero in the fourth part. These references presuppose an educated reader familiar with ancient history and philosophy — that is, a typical eighteenth-century reader of the educated upper class.

Another type of familiar image used by Pope in this *Essay* is the conventional symbol, archetypal or traditional. Among this class of images is the most significant circular frame, symbolic of the perfection of the whole of nature and the comprehen-

sive embrace of God's infinite love. Others are
Nature's light, or path, road, or walk (already
cited); and the golden age of the state of natural
innocence. Of lesser importance in the *Essay* are
Parnassian laurels (IV, 11), scales of justice, Book
of Fate, forbidden fruit, king on a throne covered
with a canopy, the five ages of man, and the rod
and feather, as in the brilliant epigram:

> *A Wit's a feather, and a Chief a rod;*
> *An honest Man's the noblest work of God.*
> (IV, 247-48)

Such traditional scientific periphrases (with the
usual standard epithets) as "vital flame" and
"vital breath," and dress figures as crowned mon-
arch, aproned cobbler, gowned parson, hooded friar,
scarfs and garters, and, of course, the myth of the
great chain or ladder of being belong to this cate-
gory, too. The net effect of these traditional images
is a sense of perspicuity and stability, of artless simplicity and classic universality. They answer the ex-
pectations of the poet's contemporary readers; and
thereby reinforcing the traditional theme of God's
goodness, they help induce conviction.

To conclude: From the great number of familiar,
realistic and secular images and classical allusions,
we cannot help feeling that the author of the *Essay
on Man* is a man himself speaking to educated lay-

men of his day, one who identified closely with his peers as he spoke their language and drew from their experiences in life and literature. But he is also a man with a more comprehensive soul because he was a poet who could synthesize all these common materials as well as a great variety of natural imagery in a work of art. Analysis of the imagery as a whole demonstrates that in this work the poet appears to be in complete control over the philosopher, the prerequisite of a philosophic poem.[32] Pope carefully and diligently multiplied his images, and the reason is plain — he wished to write good poetry.[33]

NOTES: IV

1. The integrating figure of antithesis and the structural images are discussed in the two preceding essays: "The Conversation and the Frame of Love: Images of Unity," and "Unity and Dialectic: The Structural Role of Antitheses."

2. Pope's use of the word *pictures*, which is like our modern *images*, may be seen in two of his letters —that to Arbuthnot, 26 July 1734, in which he indicates the method of his satire: "Precepts only apply to our Reason, which in most men is but weak: Examples are pictures, and strike the Senses, nay raise the Passions, and call in those (the strongest and most general of all motives) to the aid of reformation"; and that to Swift, 25 March 1736, in which he describes a project, never realized, of following the *Essay on Man*

with a series of epistles covering a variety of areas, human reason and science, useful and "un-useful" arts, learning: "It will conclude with a Satire against the misapplication of all these, exemplify'd by pictures, characters, and examples." [*The Correspondence of Alexander Pope*, ed. George Sherburn (Oxford: Clarendon, 1956), III, 419; IV, 5.] In short, Pope thought the use of names as significantly concrete; they brought forth pictures or images and thereby raised the passions. These comments apply particularly to the fourth epistle of the *Essay*, where Pope uses a good many names.

3. See Ray Frazer, "The Origin of the Term 'Image' " *ELH*, XXVII (1960), 160. Frazer quotes Brooks and Warren, Meyer Abrams, and Hugh Kenner for the modern definition: "the representation in poetry of any sense experience"; "a mental picture evoked by the use of metaphors, similes, and other figures of speech"; "what the words actually name. . . . A thing the writer names and introduces because its presence in the piece of writing will release and clarify meaning."

4. In "The Design" Pope confesses, "I was unable to treat this part of my subject [the 'arguments or instructions'] . . . more poetically, without sacrificing perspicuity to ornament. . . ." And later moral essays, he hopes, "will be less dry, and more susceptible of poetical ornament." [*Essay on Man*, ed. Maynard Mack (New Haven: Yale University Press, 1951), Vol. III, Pt. i, p. 8. This,

the Twickenham edition, is the text of the poem used in this discussion.]

5. *Corr.*, III, 250: ". . . and whenever you see what I am now writing you'll be convinced I would please but a few, and (if I could) make mankind less Admirers, and greater Reasoners." Warburton's note, 1751: "The poem he means is the *Essay on Man*. But he could never compass his Purpose: His readers would in spite of him *admire* his poetry, and would not understand his *reasoning*."

6. For the scientific "effluvia" of Pope's rose, see S. H. Monk, " 'Die of a Rose': *Essay on Man*, I, 199-200," *HLQ*, XXI (1958), 359-61. Monk makes clear that Pope refers to tiny corpuscles or extremely thin particles of a very piercing nature emitted by all objects. These swiftly penetrate the pores of our bodies, strike the nerves, and thereby cause sensation. For "effluvia," also see G. K. Chalmers, *PMLA*, LII (1937), 1050.

7. There are no images of mountains in Epistle I; in all of the *Essay* only four vague references to mountains appear—III, 250; IV, 74-6, 123, 127.

8. This extended metaphor may be considered evidence of Pope's experience as a practising painter. See Robert Allen, "Pope and the Sister Arts," *Pope and His Contemporaries*, ed. J. L. Clifford and L. Landa (Oxford: Clarendon, 1949), p. 87. J. H. Hagstrum also comments on this paintting image in *The Sister Arts* (Chicago: University of Chicago Press, 1958), p. 291.

9. Robert Allen also comments on this extended painting simile (*op. cit.*, pp. 87-8), suggesting "a parallel between the mysterious ends of divine creation and the combining efforts of the painter's art": "In describing as 'mysterious' the beneficent equilibrium between good and bad impulses, Pope invites the reader to find the same quality in the artist's handling of light and shade. The image is closely related to the more general one near the end of the first epistle of the *Essay*, in which mysterious nature is equated with 'art, unknown to thee,' the art, that is, of God."

10. Pope writes of grafting fruit trees, 19 February 1734/5 (?). [*Corr.*, III, 452.]

11. John Aikin, ed., *Essay on Man* (London, 1796), p. 22. But Aikin admits that some of the concluding lines of this epistle are eminently beautiful (pp. 22-3). Maynard Mack, "Wit and Poetry and Pope: Some Observations on his Imagery," *Pope and His Contemporaries*, p. 21.

12. Joseph Warton, as usual favoring sensuousness in the *Essay*, praises this section: "This passage is highly finished; such objects are more suited to the nature of poetry than abstract ideas. Every verb and epithet has here a descriptive force. We find more imagery from these lines to the end of the epistle, than in any other parts of this *Essay*." [*Essay on Pope*, II, 161; also in Warton's *Works of Pope* (London, 1797), III, 97.]

12a. In a letter to the Duchess of Marlborough, 6 August 1743 [*Corr.*, IV, 465], Pope uses a beehive image. *Cf. Essay on Man,* III, 184, 187-8.

13. Warburton's comment on III, 311ff: ". . . he hath the art of converting poetical ornament into philosophic reasoning; and of improving a simile into an analogical argument. . . ." [*An Essay on Man,* ed. William Warburton (London, 1743), p. 79.] Mack, in the Twickenham edition of the poem, notes how Pope uses the imagery of love to provide a sense of unity for this epistle: "Pope closes the [third] epistle (*cf.* its beginning—[the chain of love]) with two figures relating to the love that binds the universe. The love of the vine and elm was often cited in this connection, . . . and Newton's principle of attractive force holding the planets in their orbits was assimilated in Pope's time to older ideas of the diffusive love of God." [Vol. III, Pt. i, pp. 125-26.]

14. Aikin, *op. cit.,* p. 27. I cannot understand why Professor Reuben Brower declares the third epistle to be the dullest of the four, lacking the rich poetic texture of the first two. See his *Alexander Pope: The Poetry of Allusion* (Oxford: University Press, 1959), p. 226. Image analysis clearly supports the conclusion that the third is far more interesting than the second.

15. Joseph Warton deplores this mixed metaphor. Pope, he says, personifies Happiness (1-6), then uses the metaphor of a vegetable (7-17), and then pictures Happiness as a person once more (18). To fly and dwell, Warton declares, cannot be

applied to what was described as twining with
laurels and being reaped in harvests. [*Essay on
Pope*, II, 172: *Works of Pope*, III, 125.] This
image in lines 6-16 is briefly discussed by E.
Tuveson, "*An Essay on Man* and the Way of
Ideas," *ELH*, XXVI (1959), 375-76, in terms of
Locke's association of ideas.

16. What Pope says in a letter at the time he was
writing the *Essay on Man* suggests this method
of working in small units or blocks: "I employ
myself . . . a little in casting my eye upon the
great heap of fragments and hints before me, for
my large and almost boundless work, to remove
as much of which as is in any method, out of the
rest, is so much clearing the way: therefore it is
that I trouble you with so much transcribing."
[Pope to Fortescue, early March 1731/2 (?),
Corr., III, 271.] After an examination of Pope's
manuscripts, Professor Sherburn concludes "that
Pope worked by paragraphs or passages and that
his great problem was arranging the paragraphs
and tying them together tactfully." ["Pope at
Work," *Essays . . . to D. N. Smith*, Oxford, 1945),
pp. 55, 61.] May it not also be said—at least with
regard to the way in which he constructed the
Essay on Man—that Pope very often blocks
whole large image complexes into these paragraphs, and that, therefore, his image sense determined the length and development of the
paragraph unit? Admittedly, this inference is
made on the basis of working backward from the

finished product to the creative act. But the paragraph units that Professor Sherburn cites on page 61 appear to support this conclusion.

17. Ann Winslow has counted the lines that refer to nature—207 out of a total of 1304. "Here there are 67 motion images, 12 images of light and shade, 14 color images, 14 sound images, 4 sense impressions of heat and cold, 2 olfactory images, one of touch, 10 of form and extent, and 2 sense impressions of taste. The relatively small number of lines referring to nature in this poem is explained by the fact that *An Essay on Man* is primarily concerned with philosophy not with nature as are the *Pastorals* and *Windsor Forest*." ["Re-Evaluation of Pope's treatment of Nature," *University of Wyoming Publications*, IV (July, 1938), 22.] But elsewhere (p. 38) Miss Winslow says that in the Essay there are 544 lines describing nature. Unfortunately, Miss Winslow does not give the line references and makes it difficult for us to check these figures.

18. As pointed out by G. Wilson Knight, what Pope leaves unsaid about the angelic order may suggest a failure of imagination. That is, Pope may intellectually believe in angels, for they are required in his chain of being and in his logical argument; but he does not define them. [*The Vital Flame* (Oxford, 1939), p. 165.] Knight infers from this supposed failure that Pope was not fully committed to the great chain, and that he recognized the tentativeness of his hypothesis,

as indicated by the use of the conditional *Perhaps* in the watch and wheel imagery of I, 58. In Pope's defence against this a-historical criticism, John Locke's comments on human inability to provide a clear image of angels ought to be quoted: " . . . though we are told, that there are different Species of Angels; yet we know not how to frame distinct specifick Ideas of them; not out of any Conceit, that the Existence of more Species than one of Spirits is impossible; But because having no more simple Ideas (nor being able to frame more) applicable to such Beings, but only those few, taken from our selves, and from the Actions of our own Minds in thinking, and being delighted, and moving several parts of our Bodies; we can no otherwise distinguish in our Conceptions the several Species of Spirits, one from another, but by attributing those Operations and Powers, we find in ourselves, to them in a higher or lower degree; and so have no very distinct specifick Ideas of Spirits, except only of God, to whom we attribute both Duration, and all those other Ideas with Infinity; to the other Spirits with limitation. . . ." [*An Essay concerning Human Understanding* (London [5th Edition], 1706), III, vi, 11, p. 380.]

19. Professor Mack briefly touches on this function of Pope's imagery: "In the *Essay on Man*, the objects that Pope assimilates—weeds, oaks, spiders, bees, halcyons, lawns, floods, roses, rills—are held in place by their relation and meaning to

a divine and universal plan," . . . to a "sense of the metaphysical order in the world." [Twickenham ed., Vol. III, Pt. i, p. lxxv.] In only one other place does Mack again mention the way in which Pope uses imagery—in this instance Pope's use of imagery to develop the theme of the equilibrium of opposites, the unity and diversity of nature, or the *concors discordia*. [See Vol. III, Pt. i, p. lv.] For additional comment on Pope's perceptions as "unified entities," integral parts of a larger plan, see Ann Winslow, *op. cit.*, pp. 21, 39.

20. *Cf.* Geoffrey Tillotson, *Pope and Human Nature* (Oxford: University Press, 1958), pp. 122, 134: "If he gives us an individual, it is usually as a member of his group," and if he speaks of individuals, it is "not for their own sake but for the sake of coming to generalize, if possible, on the wide scale of Nature."

21. *Cf.* Tillotson again: Pope's description is not pure, "being not only picture but the medium for Nature." [*Ibid.*, p. 93.]

22. This may be exaggerated. See Pope's letter to Arbuthnot, 2 August 1734, *Corr.*, III, 424: "I write this from the most beautiful Top of a Hill I ever saw, a little house that overlooks the Sea, Southampton, & the Isle of Wight. . . ." Pope seems to refer to a fairly high, perhaps precipitous, hill overlooking the sea. See note 7 for mountains.

23. Pope's epithets, it must be noted, are supported by classical precedent. The argument in favor of

this method of writing is presented by George
Sherburn in "Pope and 'The Great Shew of
Nature'," *The Seventeenth Century: Studies in
the History of English Thought and Literature
from Bacon to Pope* by R. F. Jones, *et al.* (Stanford: Stanford University Press, 1951), p. 307.
Sherburn quotes from the *Essay on Pope's
Odyssey* (1727) wherein Joseph Spence discusses
epithets as a poetic device anad mentions Pope's
practice: "Epithets . . . like Pictures in Miniature,
are often entire descriptions in one Word. This
may be either from their own significance, or by
their immediate connexion with some known object. We see the thing, when the Poet only mentions the *Nodding Crest* of an Hero; and form a
larger Idea of *Jove* from the single Epithet of
Cloud-compelling, than we might find in a description more diffuse. . . . When *Apollo* is call'd
Archer-God, it recalls to our memory the rep-
resentations we have so often seen of that Deity:
the compleat Figure is rais'd up in the Mind, by
touching upon that single circumstance. 'Tis by
the same means, that one single Epithet gives us
the Idea of any Object, which has been common
and familiar to us. Meadows, Fields, Woods,
Rivers, and the Sea itself, are often imag'd by
one well-chosen word. Thus in that beautiful Description of Calypso's Bower, you see the Groves of
living green; the Alders *ever quivering;* the *nodding* Cypress, and its high branches, *waving* with
the Storm: 'Tis by Epithets that the ancient Poets

paint their *Elysian Groves:* and the Modern, their *Windsor-Forests.*" Spence may have developed these remarks from Pope's explanation of this practice in his "Postscript" to the *Odyssey* (1726). There Pope writes that epithets permit the poet to purify the image of possible "vulgarity or trifling" and at the same time to deal with "little circumstances," "particulars" that "are proper, and enliven the image." The poet like the painter will thus employ those details "which contribute to form a full, and yet not a confused, idea of a thing. *Epithets* are of vast service to this effect, and the right use of these is often the only expedient to render the narration poetical." He apparently saw the need for such a method of writing in order to differentiate poetry from prose. [*The Odyssey of Homer,* trans. A. Pope (London, 1726), V, 238.]

24. As a rule, Pope does not, unlike Wordsworth, develop personal and subjective imagery, as Professor Mack has noted. [Twickenham ed., Vol. III, Pt. i, p. lxxv.]

25. Perhaps the only other references are made to sunlight, sunshine, and flames: I, 131, 139, 142, 152; II, 65, 148; IV, 9, 10, 305.

26. "In the country, Pope still had his eye on man, or on man's work," Tillotson remarks, and that was why he admired Denham's *Cooper's Hill.* Tillotson even finds evidence of Pope's moral view in the *Pastorals,* and he refers us to Pope's note to the *Iliad,* XVI, 466. [*Pope and Human Nature,*

p. 103.] "Truth of description, like all other aspects of truth," John Butt writes, "Pope reserved to strengthen his moral purpose." ["The Inspiration of Pope's Poetry," *Essays . . . to D. N. Smith* (Oxford: The University Press, 1945), p. 67.] Perhaps this is the reason that Wordsworth (at least in his more tolerant moods) enjoyed Pope: "We see that Pope, by the pwer of verse alone, has contrived to render the plainest commonsense interesting, and even frequently to invest it with the appearance of passion." [*Prose Works of William Wordsworth*, ed. William Knight (London, 1896), I, 69.] See also Frederick S. Troy, "Pope's Images of Man," *Massachusetts Review*, I (Winter, 1960), 375, where the same conclusion about the *Essay on Man* is reached: "The imagery, in general, is expository rather than poetically functional: it serves to illustrate and point up the conceptual rather than to carry or dramatize personal emotion."

27. Dobrée, *English Literature in the Early 18th Century* (Oxford: the University Press, 1959), pp. 544, 546.

28. *Cf.* Tillotson, *Pope and Human Nature*, p. 141.

29. Joseph Warton deplores certain violations of propriety because they conflict with the dignified tone of the serious discourse. He cites the following passages for their "strokes of levity, of satire, of ridicule": IV, 170-71, 204-5, 223-24, 276-77. [*Essay on Pope*, II, 174-75; *Works of Pope*, III, 140.] Samuel Johnson also noted its "vulgarity

of sentiment." [*Lives of the Poets*, ed. G. B. Hill (Oxford, 1905), III, 243.] W. J. Cameron believes the choice of the word "maze" in I, 6, suggests a kind of flippancy that undermines serious commitment. [" 'Doctrinal to an Age': Pope's Essay on Man," *Dublin Review*, CCXXV (1951, 2nd Quarter), 65.] Others, such as Roscoe—and Warton, too, have objected to the garden and hunting figures at the very beginning.

30. John Arthos cites these as scientific commonplaces in the literature of the period. [*The Language of Natural Description in 18th Century Poetry* (Ann Arbor: University of Michigan, 1949).] He also states that the following words and phrases were common expressions in scientific literature: *aether*, meaning vitalizing air or element; *wat'ry waste* (I, 106), meaning the sea; *yonder argent fields above* (I, 41), meaning the sky; *frame* (I, 267-70), meaning machine; *gen'rous* (III, 311), and *nation*. (III, 99-100)

31. Mack has commented on the way in which Pope has secularized his vindication of God's way by avoiding religious allegory; for Genesis, the Scriptural narrative of the creation, Pope has substituted the chain of being; for the Garden of Eden, the garden of temptations in the world; for Adam, the honest man; for the regaining of paradise through the coming of Christ, the inner virtue of charity and love in the happy citizen. [Twickenham ed., Vol. III, Pt. i, p. lxiv.]

32. On the two hundreth anniversary of the poet's

death, the editor of the *Times Literary Supplement* described the poet's work as "straight talking, supported with many a sprightly illustration drawn from nature or the proper study of man; never boring, and cast always in the neatest possible verse; the poet in complete control over the philosopher, which is the prerequisite of a philosophic poem." [*TLS*, 3 June 1944, p. 271.] For a completely opposite reaction, one that denies any poetic merit whatsoever to the *Essay on Man* (except to those parts that are vitalized by satire), see *TLS*, 10 August 1933, pp. 529-30. As a measure of Pope's ability to act powerfully on the imagination of sensitive and receptive readers, see John Stuart Mill's reaction as briefly noted in his *Autobiography* (London, 1873), p. 113: "In the most sectarian period of my Benthamism, I happened to look into Pope's *Essay on Man*, and though every opinion in it was contrary to mine, I well remember how powerfully it acted on my imagination."

33. Samuel Johnson wrote that it was Pope's "dilatory caution" that "enabled him to condense his sentiments, to multiply his images, and to accumulate all that study might produce, or chance might supply." [*Lives of the Poets*, III, 223.]

AN ESSAY ON MAN Image and Figure	I	II	III	IV
Nature	13, 39, 103, 133, 141, 150, 172, 179, 245, 256, 268, 289	32, 115, 145, 153, 161, 184, 195, 205, 229, 275	9, 43, 91, 117, 147-60, 163, 169, 171-98, 190, 199, 215, 236, 243, 286-8, 317,	29, 56, 78, 108, 112, 115, 166, 332, 345-50, 393
light, sun	139, 142, 271	22, 28, 203, 283	287	9, 168, 393
fire, flame			118	10
ocean, sea, tide	139, 158, 167, 233	20, 107	19-20, 101, 204	
streams, lake, spring	138, 204			364, 369
earth, soil	63, 233, 270			8, 292
mountains			250	74-6, 123, 127
pastoral scene	9-13		147-60	
vegetation, growing things		63	15-6	7-16
trees, grafting	39, 272	175-94	138, 203	
seeds			37, 118	7-8
vine			311	
grain			38	
fruit	8, 135			176
flower	7, 135, 200, 220	90		
weeds, seaweed	7, 40			292
weather (storm, wind)	143, 152-3, 155, 157-8	102	68, 249	
star	19, 21-34, 41-2, 272	21, 23, 35-7, 65	313-4	
cloud, shade, darkness		203		243, 304
air, elements	167, 204, 233	20, 111	116-7	
Animals	12-3	8	24, 57, 99, 102, 119-20, 125, 152	
domestic	61-2, 63-4, 79, 81-4, 112, 176, 214, 221, 239		35, 40, 41, 65-7	178
wild	176, 185, 212, 213, 222	34	29, 44, 64, 176	
insects	185, 194-6, 210, 217-8, 219-20	90	55, 103-4, 175, 181-8, 191	
birds	14, 88, 216, 239		31, 33, 38, 46, 53, 54, 55, 56, 57, 105, 125, 173, 222,	
fish	215, 235		58, 177	
reptiles	258	132		
Religion	99-112	27-8	6, 84, 147-60, 235-68	24, 42, 137-40, 177-8
God, Heaven, Providence	16, 17, 21-8, 50, 64, 68, 69, 77, 87, 92, 100, 104, 114-30, (118-9, 122,	1, 8, 29, 109, 116, 204, 238, 248	1-2, 22, 27, 71, 77, 98, 109, 148, 156, 224, 232-4, 237, 240, 248, 317	35, 49, 53, 69, 93, 110, 113, 117, 121, 135-6, 140, 162, 173, 248, 327, 332, 361,

AN ESSAY ON MAN Image and Figure	I	II	III	IV
angels, spirits	126-7, 130), 145, 155, 163, 186, 196, 203, 205, 237, 255-6, 266-8, 279-80, 284, 287			372
Bible	79, 91, 110, 126-8, 174, 238, 253, 278	109, 132, 203-4		118, 312
Science				
astronomy	19, 21, 23-31, 41-4, 89-90, 101-2, 131, 150, 240, 283	19-43		128
frame	29-34, 264, 270	137	111, 317	
circle, sphere, wheel	26, 53-9, 72-3, 86, 101, 124, 202, 247-56, 285	19-30, 35-7, 65	301-2, 313-6	363-72
chain of being and love	31-4, 45-8, 113, 173-258		7-26, 114, 129, 133, 150	288, 333-40
alchemy		111-6, 147-8 175-94, 269		
humors psychology		139, 159		
misc. scientific references	199 (effluvia)	115-8 (aether, vital, genial), 231 (prism), 34-8 (Newton)	104 (Demoivre)	
Other Learning				
law		155-6		187, 250-2
classical myth	202	270		11,375
ancient history	156, 159, 160	198-200		146-8, 208, 220, 244, 246, 257-8
modern history	156			99, 100, 101-4, 107, 130, 216, 220, 244, 246, 250, 260-6, 281, 284
philosophy		5-6, 23-6, 81-6, 101		123-4, 235-6, 240
geography		3, 221-30		246, 292, 295
Domestic				
social classes		241-70		
clothes and jewels		44-5, 279		10, 171, 196-204
money, property	108	279	4	76, 85-6, 170, 187, 192, 269-76, 279, 296, 306-8
food		90, 148		150, 176, 205

AN ESSAY ON MAN Image and Figure	I	II	III	IV
Body				
bodily action, body	180, 259-62, 276	9		237
sickness, medicine	142, 155, 220	133-44, 159-60	165	108, 119-20
facial features				224
drink, thirst	136	288		
senses	193-6, 197-8, 199-200, 201-4			
Daily Life				
watches, clocks	53-9	59-60		
pulley, strainer		189		293-4
scale	113-22			69
games and hunting	9-13, 117	17, 197		
military, war, engines	262		85-90, 107-8, 268	12, 153-4, 171, 247
politics, royalty	2, 140	149	148, 209-14	9, 41, 121-2, 172, 187, 205-6, 277, 289
toys		276, 282		180
navigation, roads		105-10, 161, 165-8		29, 40, 331, 379-86
Arts				
visual		117-22, 208-10, 213-4, 283-6		303-4
musical	291		290-6	
landscape gardening	5-14			304
Imaginative				
personification	13, 92, 204	42-6, 100, 117-8, 143, 145, 217-20, 271-4, 282, 283, 286, 288	246-60	1-5, 15-8, 63, 67, 79, 82, 83, 87-90, 149-51, 154, 168-9, 319-20, 341, 371-2, 383, 393